# Facility Integrated
# Contingency Planning

# Facility Integrated Contingency Planning

## For Emergency Response and Planning

*Thomas M. Socha*

Writers Club Press
San Jose  New York  Lincoln  Shanghai

Facility Integrated Contingency Planning
For Emergency Response and Planning

Writers Club Press
an imprint of iUniverse, Inc.

For information address:
iUniverse, Inc.
5220 S. 16th St., Suite 200
Lincoln, NE 68512
www.iuniverse.com

Always do your own research before starting a contingency plan.

ISBN: 0-595-24781-4

Printed in the United States of America

*This book is dedicated to the emergency responders and the environmental, health, and safety professionals.*

# Contents

# List of Abbreviations

ACP: Area Contingency Plan

ASTM: American Society of Testing Materials

bbls: Barrels

bpd: Barrels per Day

bph: Barrels per Hour

CHRIS: Chemical Hazards Response Information System

COTP: Captain of the Port

CWA: Clean Water Act

DOI: Department of Interior

DOC: Department of Commerce

DOT: Department of Transportation

EPA: Environmental Protection Agency

FEMA: Federal Emergency Management Agency

FR: Federal Register

gal: Gallons

gpm: Gallons per Minute

HAZMAT: Hazardous Materials

IC: Incident Commander

ICP: Integrated Contingency Plan or Incident Command Plan

ICS: Incident Command System

LEPC: Local Emergency Planning Committee

MMS: Minerals Management Service (part of DOI)

NCP: National Oil and Hazardous Substances Pollution Contingency Plan

NOAA: National Oceanic and Atmospheric Administration (part of DOC)

NIIMS: National Interagency Incident Management System

NCP: National Oil and Hazardous Substances Pollution Contingency Plan, 40 CFR Part 300

NPFC: National Pollution Fund Center

NRC: National Response Center

NRT: National Response Team

OPA: Oil Pollution Act of 1990

OSC: On-Scene Coordinator

OSLTF: Oil Spill Liability Trust Fund

PREP: National Preparedness for Response Exercise Program

RA: Regional Administrator

RCRA: Resource Conservation and Recovery Act

RRC: Regional Response Centers

RP: Responsible Party

RRT: Regional Response Team

RSPA: Research and Special Programs Administration

SARA: Superfund Amendments and Reauthorization Act

SERC: State Emergency Response Commission

SDWA: Safe Drinking Water Act of 1986

SI: Surface Impoundment

SIC: Standard Industrial Classification

SPCC: Spill Prevention, Control, and Countermeasures

USCG: United States Coast Guard

# Chapter 1

## The Integrated Contingency Plan

## 1.0 Plan Introduction

*Integrated Contingency Plan*

The ICP will minimize duplication in the preparation and use of emergency response plans at the same facility and will improve economic efficiency for both the regulated and regulating communities. Facility expenditures for the preparation, maintenance, submission, and update of a single plan should be much lower than for multiple plans.

The use of a single emergency response plan per facility will eliminate confusion for facility first responders who often must decide which of their plans is applicable to a particular emergency. The guidance is designed to yield a highly functional document for use in varied emergency situations while providing a mechanism for complying with multiple agency requirements. Use of a single integrated plan should also improve coordination between facility response personnel and local, state, and federal emergency response personnel.

The adoption of a standard plan format should facilitate integration of plans within a facility, in the event that large facilities may need to prepare separate plans for distinct operating units. The ICP concept should also allow coordination of facility plans with plans that are maintained by local emergency planning committees (LEPCs), [1]Area Committees, [2]co-operatives, and mutual aid organizations. In some cases, there are specific regulatory requirements to ensure that facility plans are consistent with external planning efforts. Industry use of this guidance along with active participation on local and Area Committees will improve the level of emergency preparedness and is therefore highly encouraged.

In some areas, it may be possible to go beyond simple coordination of plans and actually integrate certain information from facility plans with corresponding areas of external plans. The adoption of a single, common ICP outline such as the one proposed in this guidance would facilitate a move toward integration of facility plans with local, state, and federal plans.

The projected results described above will ultimately serve the mutual goal of the response community to more efficiently and effectively protect public health, worker safety, the environment, and property.

[1] LEPC plans are developed by LEPCs in coordination with facility emergency response coordinators under section 303 of the Emergency Planning and Community Right-to-Know Act.

[2] Area Contingency Plans are developed by Area Committees pursuant to section 4202(a)(6) of the Oil Pollution Act of 1990 (OPA).

*Organizational Concepts*

The ICP format provided in this one-plan guidance (See 1.0.1) is organized into three main sections: an introductory section, a core plan, and a series of supporting annexes. It is important to note that the elements contained in these sections are not new concepts, but accepted emergency response activities that are currently addressed in various forms in existing contingency planning regulations. The goal of the National Response Team (NRT) is not to create new planning requirements, but to provide a mechanism to consolidate existing concepts into a single functional plan structure. This approach would provide a consistent basis for addressing emergency response concerns as it gains widespread use among facilities.

The introduction section of the plan format is designed to provide facility response personnel, outside responders, and regulatory officials with basic information about the plan and the entity it covers. It calls for a statement of purpose and scope, a table of contents, information on the current revision date of the plan, general facility information, and the key contact(s) for plan development and maintenance. This section should present the information in a brief factual manner.

The structure of the sample core plan and annexes in this guidance is based on the structure of the National Interagency Incident Management System (NIIMS) Incident Command System (ICS). NIIMS ICS is a nationally recognized system currently in use by numerous federal, state, and local organizations (e.g., some Area Committees under OPA).

NIIMS ICS is a type of response management system that has been used successfully in a variety of emergency situations, including releases of oil or hazardous substances. NIIMS ICS provides a commonly understood framework that allows for effective interaction among response personnel. Organizing the ICP along the lines of the NIIMS ICS will allow the plan to dovetail with established response management practices, thus facilitating its ease of use during an emergency.

The core plan is intended to contain essential response guidance and procedures. Annexes would contain more detailed supporting information on specific response management functions. The core plan should contain frequent references to the response critical annexes to direct response personnel to parts of the ICP that contain more detailed information on the appropriate course of action for responders to take during various stages of a response. Facility planners need to find the right balance between the amount of information contained in the core plan versus the response critical annexes (Annexes 1 through 3). Information required to support response actions at facilities with multiple hazards will likely be contained in the annexes. Planners at facilities with fewer hazards may choose to include most if not all information in the core plan. Other annexes (e.g., Annexes 4 through 8) are dedicated to providing information that is non-critical at the time of a response (e.g., cross-references to demonstrate regulatory compliance and background planning information). Consistent with the goal of keeping the size of the ICP as manageable as practicable, it is not necessary for a plan holder to provide its field responders with all the compliance documentation (e.g., Annexes 4 through 8) that it submits to regulatory agencies. Similarly, it may not be necessary for a plan holder to submit all annexes to every regulatory agency for review.

Basic headings are consistent across the core plan and annexes to facilitate ease of use during an emergency. These headings provide a comprehensive list of elements to be addressed in the core plan and response annexes and may not be relevant to all facilities. Planners should address those regulatory elements that are applicable to their particular facilities. Planners at facilities with multiple hazards will need to address most, if not all, elements included in this guidance. Planners at facilities with fewer hazards may not need to address certain elements. If planners choose to strictly adopt the ICP outline contained in this guidance but are not required by regulation to address all elements of the outline, they may simply indicate "not applicable" for those items where no information is provided. A more detailed discussion of the core plan and supporting annexes follows.

## 1.0.1 ICP Outline

### Section I—Plan Introduction Elementss

1. Purpose and Scope of Plan Coverage
2. Table of Contents
3. Current Revision Date
4. General Facility Identification Information
a. Facility name
b. Owner/operator/agent (include physical and mailing address and phone number)
c. Physical address of the facility (include county/parish/borough, latitude/longitude, and directions)
d. Mailing address of the facility (correspondence contact)
e. Other identifying information (e.g., ID numbers, SIC Code, oil storage start-up date)
f. Key contact(s) for plan development and maintenance
g. Phone number for key contact(s)
h. Facility phone number
i. Facility fax number

### Section II—Core Plan Elementss

1. Discovery

2. Initial Response
a. Procedures for internal and external notifications (i.e., contact, organization name, and phone number of facility emergency response coordinator, facility response team personnel, federal, state, and local officials)
b. Establishment of a response management system
c. Procedures for preliminary assessment of the situation, including an identification of incident type, hazards involved, magnitude of the problem, and resources threatened

d. Procedures for establishment of objectives and priorities for response to the specific incident, including:
(1) Immediate goals/tactical planning (e.g., protection of workers and public as priorities)
(2) Mitigating actions (e.g., discharge/release control, containment, and recovery, as appropriate)
(3) Identification of resources required for response
e. Procedures for implementation of tactical plan
f. Procedure for mobilization of resources

3. Sustained Actions

4. Termination and Follow-Up Actions

**Section III-Annexes**

Annex 1. Facility and Locality Information

a. Facility maps
b. Facility drawings
c. Facility description/layout, including identification of facility hazards and vulnerable resources and populations on and off the facility which may be impacted by an incident

Annex 2. Notification

a. Internal notifications
b. Community notifications
c. Federal and state agency notifications

Annex 3. Response Management System

a. General

b. Command
(1) List facility Incident Commander and Qualified Individual (if applicable) by name and/or title and provide information on their authorities and duties
(2) Information (i.e., internal and external communications)
(3) Safety
(4) Liaison—Staff mobilizationn

c. Operations
(1) Operational response objectives
(2) Discharge or release control
(3) Assessment/monitoring
(4) Containment
(5) Recovery
(6) Decontamination
(7) Non-responder medical needs including information on ambulances and hospitals
(8) Salvage plans

d. Planning
(1) Hazard assessment, including facility hazards identification, vulnerability analysis, and prioritization of potential risks
(2) Protection
(3) Coordination with natural resource trustees
(4) Waste management

e. Logistics
(1) Medical needs of responders
(2) Site security
(3) Communications (internal and external resources)
(4) Transportation (air, land, water)
(5) Personnel support (e.g., meals, housing, equipment)
(6) Equipment maintenance and support

f. Finance/procurement/administration
(1) Resource list
(2) Personnel management
(3) Response equipment
(4) Support equipment
(5) Contracting
(6) Claims procedures
(7) Cost documentation

Annex 4. Incident Documentation

a. Post accident investigation
b. Incident history

Annex 5. Training and Exercises/Drills

Annex 6. Response Critique and Plan Review and Modification Process

Annex 7. Prevention

Annex 8. Regulatory Compliance and Cross-Reference Matrices

# 1.1 Purpose and Scope of Plan Coverage

This Section includes the following regulations:

| RCRA (40 CFR part 264, Subpart D, 40 CFR Part 265, Subpart D, and 40 CFR 279.52 | EPA's Oil Pollution Prevention Regulation (40 CFR Part 112) | USCG-FRG (33 CFR Part 154) | DOT/RSP A-FRP (49 CFR part 194) | OSHA Emergency Action Plans (29 CFR 1910.38(a)) and Process Safety (29 CFR 1910.119) | OSHA HAZWOPER (29 CFR 1910.120) | CAA RMP (40 CFR part 68) |
|---|---|---|---|---|---|---|
| 264.51 265.51 279.52(b)(1) 264.52(a) 265.52(a) 279.52(b)(2)(i) | | | | 38(a) 119(n) 272(d) | (l) (p)(8) (q)(1) | |

This section provides a brief overview of facility operations and describes in general the physical area, and nature of hazards or events to which the plan is applicable. This brief description will help plan users to quickly assess the relevancy of the plan to a particular type of emergency in a given location. This section also includes a list of which regulation(s) that are being addressed in the ICP.

The U.S. Environmental Protection Agency is providing a mechanism for consolidating multiple plans through the National Response Team (NRT) in which facilities may have prepared to comply with various regulations into one functional emergency response plan or integrated contingency plan (ICP).

*Each owner or operator* **must** have a contingency plan for his facility. The contingency plan **must** be designed to minimize hazards to human health or the environment from fires, explosions, or any unplanned sudden or non-sudden releases of hazardous waste or hazardous waste constituents to air, soil, or surface water (40 CFR 264.51(a)).

*The integrated contingency plan* **must** describe the actions facility personnel **must** take to fires, explosions, or any unplanned sudden or non-sudden release of used oil to air, soil, or surface water at the facility. (40 279.52 (b) (2) (i)). The provisions of the plan **must** be carried out immediately whenever there is a fire, explosion, or release of hazardous waste or hazardous waste constituents which could threaten human health or the environment (40 CFR 264.51(b)).

*The employer* **shall** *establish and implement* an emergency action plan for the entire plant in accordance with the provisions of 29 CFR 1910.38(a). In addition, the emergency action plan *shall* include procedures for handling small releases.

*The emergency action plan* **shall** be in writing and available for inspection and copying by employees, their representatives, OSHA personnel and other governmental agencies with responsibilities.

Also, the *owner or operator* **shall** develop and implement an emergency response program for the purpose of protecting public health and the environment. Such program *shall* include the following elements:

- An emergency response plan, which *shall* be maintained at the stationary source and other ICP facilities. The plan **must** contain at least the following elements:
a. Procedures for informing the public and local emergency response agencies about accidental releases;
b. Documentation of proper first-aid and emergency medical treatment necessary to treat accidental human exposures; and
c. Procedures and measures for emergency response after an accidental release of a regulated substance;
- Procedures for the use of emergency response equipment and for its inspection, testing, and maintenance;

- Training for all employees in relevant procedures; and
- Procedures to review and update, as appropriate, the emergency response plan to reflect changes at the stationary source and ensure that employees are informed of changes (40 CFR 68.95 (a)(1)-(a)(4)).

The emergency response plan developed under paragraph 40 CFR 68.95(a) (1) *shall* be coordinated with the community emergency response plan developed under 42 U.S.C. 11003. Upon request of the local emergency planning committee or emergency response officials, the owner or operator *shall* promptly provide to the local emergency response officials information necessary for developing and implementing the community emergency response plan.

Since this an example of a plan; it follows:

- EPA's Oil Pollution Prevention Regulation (SPCC and Facility Response Plan Requirements)—40 CFR part 112.7(d) and 112.20-.21;
- EPA's Risk Management Programs Regulation—40 CFR part 68;
- EPA's Resource Conservation and Recovery Act Contingency Planning Requirements—40 CFR part 264, Subpart D, 40 CFR part 265, Subpart D, and 40 CFR
- MMS's Facility Response Plan Regulation-30 CFR part 254;
- RSPA's Pipeline Response Plan Regulation—49 CFR part 194;
- USCG's Facility Response Plan Regulation—33 CFR part 154, Subpart F;
- OSHA's Emergency Action Plan Regulation—29 CFR 1910.38(a);
- OSHA's Process Safety Standard—29 CFR 1910.119; and
- OSHA's HAZWOPER Regulation—29 CFR 1910.120.

## 1.2 Table of Contents

This section should clearly identify the structure of the plan and include a list of annexes. This will facilitate rapid use of the plan during an emergency.

| RCRA (40 CFR part 264, Subpart D, 40 CFR Part 265, Subpart D, and 40 CFR 279.52 | EPA's Oil Pollution Prevention Regulation (40 CFR Part 112) | USCG-FRG (33 CFR Part 154) | DOT/RSPA-FRP (49 CFR part 194) |
|---|---|---|---|
|  | 112.20(h) Appendix F | 1035(a)(4) 1030(b) | Appendix A |

## 1.3 Current Revision Date

This section should indicate the date that the plan was last revised to provide plan users with information on the currency of the plan. More detailed information on plan update history (i.e., a record of amendments) may be maintained in Annex 6 (Response Critique and Plan Review and Modification Process).

| RCRA (40 CFR part 264, Subpart D, 40 CFR Part 265, Subpart D, and 40 CFR 279.52 | EPA's Oil Pollution Prevention Regulation (40 CFR Part 112) | USCG-FRG (33 CFR Part 154) | DOT/RSP A-FRP (49 CFR part 194) | OSHA Emergency Action Plans (29 CFR 1910.38(a)) and Process Safety (29 CFR 1910.119) | OSHA HAZWO PER (29 CFR 1910.120) | CAA RMP (40 CFR part 68) |
|---|---|---|---|---|---|---|
|  | F1.2 | 1035(a)(6) |  |  |  |  |

## 1.4 General Facility Identification Information

This section should contain a brief profile of the facility and its key personnel to facilitate rapid identification of key administrative information.

| RCRA (40 CFR part 264, Subpart D, 40 CFR Part 265, Subpart D, and 40 CFR 279.52 | EPA's Oil Pollution Prevention Regulation (40 CFR Part 112) | USCG-FRG (33 CFR Part 154) | DOT/RSPA-FRP (49 CFR part 194) | OSHA Emergency Action Plans (29 CFR 1910.38(a)) and Process Safety (29 CFR 1910.119) | OSHA HAZWOPER (29 CFR 1910.120) | CAA RMP (40 CFR part 68) |
|---|---|---|---|---|---|---|
| | 112.20(h)(2) F1.2 F1.9 F2.0 F2.1 | 1035(a)(1) 1035(a)(2) 1035(a)(3) 1035(e) | 194.107(d)(1)(i) 194.113 194.113(a)(1) 194.113(b)(1) 194.113(b)(3),(4) A-1 | 38(a)(2)(vi) | (l)(2)(i),(ii) (p)(8)(ii)(A),(B) (q)(2)(i),(ii) | |

a.    Facility name: _____

b.    Owner/operator/agent (include physical and mailing address and phone number):

      Name:
      Phone Number:
      Address:
      City:
      County/Parish/Borough:
      State:
      Zip Code:

c.    Physical address of the facility (include county/parish/borough, latitude/longitude, and directions):

      Address:
      City:
      County/Parish/Borough:
      State:
      Zip Code:
      Latitude/Longitude:

      Directions:

      _____
      _____
      _____

d.    Mailing address of the facility (correspondence contract)

| Attn: | Thomas Socha |
|---|---|
| Address: | 2130 Somewhere Drive |
| City: | Nowhereville |
| County/Parish/Borough: | Oakland |
| State: | Michigan |
| Zip Code: | 48888-8888 |

e. Other identifying information (e.g., ID numbers, SIC code, and oil storage startup date)
f. Key contact(s) for plan development and maintenance
g. Phone number(s) for key contact(s) and Qualified Individual(s)
h. Facility phone number
I. Facility fax number

# Chapter 2

## *The Essential Process*

### 2.0 Core Plan Elements

The core plan is intended to reflect the essential steps necessary to initiate, conduct, and terminate an emergency response action: recognition, notification, and initial response, including assessment, mobilization, and implementation. This section of the plan should be concise and easy to follow. A rule of thumb is that the core plan should fit in the glovebox of a response vehicle. The core plan need not detail all procedures necessary under these phases of a response but should provide information that is time critical in the earliest stages of a response and a framework to guide responders through key steps necessary to mount an effective response. The response action section should be convenient to use and understandable at the appropriate skill level.

The NRT recommends the use of checklists or flowcharts wherever possible to capture these steps in a concise easy-to-understand manner. The core plan should be constructed to contain references to appropriate sections of the supporting annexes for more detailed guidance on specific procedures. The NRT anticipates that for a large, complex facility with multiple hazards the annexes will contain a significant amount of information on specific procedures to follow. For a small facility with a limited number of hazard scenarios, the core plan may contain most if not all of the information necessary to carry out the response thus obviating the need for more detailed annexes. The checklists, depending on their size and complexity, can be in either the core or the support section.

The core plan should reflect a hierarchy of emergency response levels. A system of response levels is commonly used in emergency planning for classifying emergencies according to seriousness and assigning an appropriate standard response or series of response actions to each level. Both complex and simple industrial facilities use a system of response levels for rapidly assessing the seriousness of an emergency and developing an appropriate response. This process allows response personnel to match the emergency and its potential impacts with appropriate resources and personnel. The concept of response levels should be considered in developing checklists or flowcharts designed to serve as the basis for the core plan. Note that for those facilities subject to planning requirements under OPA, response levels in the core plan may not necessarily correspond to discharge planning amounts (e.g., average most probable discharge, maximum most probable discharge, and worst case discharge).

Facility owners and operators should determine appropriate response levels based on 1) the need to initiate time-urgent response actions to minimize or prevent unacceptable consequences to the health and safety of workers, the public, or the environment; and 2) the need to communicate critical information concerning the emergency to offsite authorities. The consideration and development of response levels should, to the extent practicable, be consistent with similar efforts that may have been taken by the LEPC, local Area Committee, or mutual aid organization. Response levels, which are used in communications with offsite authorities, should be fully coordinated and use consistent terminology.

## 2.0.1 Discovery

| RCRA (40 CFR part 264, Subpart D, 40 CFR Part 265, Subpart D, and 40 CFR 279.52 | EPA's Oil Pollution Prevention Regulation (40 CFR Part 112) | USCG-FRG (33 CFR Part 154) | DOT/RSPA-FRP (49 CFR part 194) | OSHA Emergency Action Plans (29 CFR 1910.38(a)) and Process Safety (29 CFR 1910.119) | OSHA HAZWOPER (29 CFR 1910.120) | CAA RMP (40 CFR part 68) |
|---|---|---|---|---|---|---|
| | 112.20(h)(6) F1.6.1, F1.6.2 | 1035(b)(3)(i) | 194.107(d)(1) (iii) A-3 | 119(n) | (l)(2)(iii) (p)(8)(iii)(C) (q)(2)(iii) | 68.95(a) (1)(iii) |

This section addresses the initial action the person(s) discovering an incident will take to assess the problem at hand and access the response system. Recognition, basic assessment, source control (as appropriate), and initial notification of proper personnel should be addressed in a manner that can be easily understood by everybody in the facility. The checklists or flowcharts are highly recommended. This section includes the following procedures for spill detection and on-scene spill mitigation:

• Methods of initial discharge detection which include:

(a) The facility owners or operators *shall* describe the procedures and personnel that will detect any spill or uncontrolled discharge of oil or release of a hazardous substance. A thorough discussion of facility inspections **must** be included. In addition, a description of initial response actions *shall* be addressed. This section *shall* reference section 40 CFR, Appendix 1.3.1 or (section 2.1.2 of this ICP) of the response plan for emergency response information (40 CFR 112, Appendix F 1.6.1).

(b) The facility owners or operators **must** describe any automated spill detection equipment that the facility has in place. This section *shall* include a discussion of overfill alarms, secondary containment sensors, etc. A discussion of the plans to verify an automated alarm and the actions to be taken once verified **must** also be included (40 CFR 112, Appendix F 1.6.2).

- Procedures, listed in the order of priority, that personnel are required to follow in responding to a pipeline, release, and spill emergency to mitigate or prevent any discharge from the pipeline, release, and spill;
- A list of equipment that may be needed in response activities on land and navigable waters, including—

(1) Transfer hoses and connection equipment;
(2) Portable pumps and ancillary equipment; and
(3) Facilities available to transport and receive oil from a leaking pipeline;
- Identification of the availability, location, and contact telephone numbers to obtain equipment for response activities on a 24-hour basis; and
- Identification of personnel and their location, telephone numbers, and responsibilities for use of equipment in response activities on a 24-hour basis (49 CFR 194, Appendix A-3).

## 2.1 Initial Response

This section should provide for activation of the response system following discovery of the incident. It should include an established 24-hour contact point (i.e., that person and alternate who is called to set the response in motion) and instructions for that person on who to call and what critical information to pass. Plan drafters should also consider the need for bilingual notification. It is important to note that different incident types require that different parties be notified. Appropriate federal, State, and local notification requirements should be reflected in this section of the ICP. Detailed notification lists may be included here or in Annex 2, depending upon the variety of notification schemes that a facility may need to implement. For example, the release of an extremely hazardous substance will require more extensive notifications (i.e., to State Emergency Response Commissions (SERCs) and LEPCs) than a discharge of oil. Even though no impacts or awareness are anticipated outside the site, immediate external notifications are required for releases of CERCLA and EPCRA substances. Again, the use of forms, such as flowcharts, checklists, call-down lists, is recommended.

This section should instruct personnel in the implementation of a response management system for coordinating the response effort. More detailed information on specific components and functions of the response management system (e.g., detailed hazard assessment, resource protection strategies) may be provided in annexes to the ICP.

This part of the plan should then provide information on problem assessment, establishment of objectives and priorities, implementation of a tactical plan, and mobilization of resources. In establishing objectives and priorities for response, facilities should perform a hazard assessment using resources such as Material Safety Data Sheets (MSDSs) or the Chemical Hazard Response Information System (CHRIS) manual. Hazardous Materials Emergency Planning Guide (NRT-1), developed by the NRT to assist community personnel with emergency response planning, provides guidance on developing hazard analyses. If a facility elects to provide detailed hazard analysis information in a response annex, then a reference to that annex should be provided in this part of the core plan.

Mitigating actions must be tailored to the type of hazard present. For example, containment might be applicable to an oil spill (i.e., use of booming strategies) but would not be relevant to a gas release. The plan holder is encouraged to develop checklists, flowcharts, and brief descriptions of actions to be taken to control different types of incidents. Relevant questions to ask in developing such materials include:

- What type of emergency is occurring?
- What areas/resources have been or will be affected?
- Do we need an exclusion zone?

- Is the source under control?
- What type of response resources are needed?

| EPA's Oil Pollution Prevention Regulation (40 CFR Part 112) | USCG-FRG (33 CFR Part 154) | DOT/RS PA-FRP (49 CFR part 194) | OSHA Emergency Action Plans (29 CFR 1910.38(a)) and Process Safety (29 CFR 1910.119) | OSHA HAZWOPER (29 CFR 1910.120) | CAA RMP (40 CFR part 68) |
|---|---|---|---|---|---|
| 112.20(h)(7)(i) F1.3.6 F1.7 | 1035(b)(2)(ii) 1035(b)(3)(i) 1035(b)(3)(ii) | A-2 | 38(a)(2)(i) 38(a)(2)(ii) 119(n) | (l)(2)(iii) (p)(8)(iii)(C) (q)(2)(iii) | 68.95(a)(1)(iii) |

## EPA's Oil Pollution Prevention Regulation

The facility owners or operators **must** explain in detail how to implement the facility's emergency response plan by describing response actions to be carried out under the plan to ensure the safety of the facility and to mitigate or prevent discharges described in (40CFR 112, Appendix 1.5) of the response plan. This section *shall* include the identification of response resources for small, medium, and worst case spills; disposal plans; and containment and drainage planning. A list of those personnel who would be involved in the cleanup *shall* be identified. Procedures that the facility will use, where appropriate or necessary, to update their plan after an oil spill event and the time frame to update the plan **must** be described.

## DOT/RSPA-FRP

*Notification Procedures*

- Notification requirements that apply in each area of operation of pipelines covered by the plan, including applicable State or local requirements;
- A checklist of notifications the operator or qualified individual is required to make under the response plan, listed in the order of priority;
- Names of persons (individuals or organizations) to be notified of a discharge, indicating whether notification is to be performed by operating personnel or other personnel;
- Procedures for notifying qualified individuals;
- The primary and secondary communication methods by which notifications can be made; and
- The information to be provided in the initial and each follow-up notification, including the following:

(1) Name of pipeline;

(2) Time of discharge;

(3) Location of discharge;

(4) Name of oil involved;

(5) Reason for discharge (e.g., material failure, excavation damage, and corrosion);

(6) Estimated volume of oil discharged;

(7) Weather conditions on scene; and

(8) Actions taken or planned by persons on scene.

## 2.1.1 Procedures for internal and external notifications

| RCRA (40 CFR part 264, Subpart D, 40 CFR Part 265, Subpart D, and 40 CFR 279.52 | EPA's Oil Pollution Prevention Regulation (40 CFR Part 112) | USCG-FRG (33 CFR Part 154) | DOT/RSPA-FRP (49 CFR part 194) | OSHA Emergency Action Plans (29 CFR 1910.38(a)) and Process Safety (29 CFR 1910.119) | OSHA HAZWOP ER (29 CFR 1910.120) | CAA RMP (40 CFR part 68) |
|---|---|---|---|---|---|---|
| 264.52(d) 265.52(d) 279.52(b)(2)(iv) 264.55 265.55 279.52(b)(5) 264.56(a)(1),(2) 265.56(a)(1),(2) 279.52(b)(6)(i)(A),(B) 264.56(d)(1),(2) 265.56(d)(1),(2) 279.52(b)(6)(iv)(A),(B) | 112.20(h)(1)(iii) 112.20(h)(3)(iii) 112.20(h)(3)(iv) F1.2 F1.3.1 | 1026 1035(a)(3) 1035(b)(1)(i) 1035(e)(2) | 194.107(d)(1) (ii) 194.113(b)(2) A-1, A-1(b)(2) A-2 A-5 | 38(a)(2)(v) 38(a)(2)(vi) 38(a)(3)(i) 38(a)(3)(ii) 165 | (l)(2)(ix) (p)(8)(ii)(I) (q)(2)(ix) | 68.95(a)(1) (i) |

The plan **must** list names, addresses, and phone numbers (office and home) of all persons qualified to act as emergency coordinator (see Sec. 2.3.1 of the ICP), and this list **must** be kept up to date. Where more than one person is listed, one **must** be named as primary emergency coordinator and others **must** be listed in the order in which they will assume responsibility as alternates. For new facilities, this information **must** be supplied to the Regional Administrator at the time of certification, rather than at the time of permit application (40 CFR 264.52(d)).

## 2.1.2 Notification

Date of Last Update: _____

### 2.1.2.1 Emergency Notification Phone List Whom to Notify

**Reporter's Name:**
**Date:**
**Facility Name:**
**Owner Name:**
**Facility Identification Number:**
**Date and Time of Each NRC Notification:**

| Organization | Phone Number |
|---|---|
| 1. Qualified Individual:<br>Evening Phone: | |
| 2. National Response Center (NRC): | 1-800-424-8802 |
| 3. Company Response Team:<br>Evening Phone: | |
| 4. Federal On-Scene Coordinator (OSC) and/or Regional Response Center (RRC):<br>Evening Phone:<br>Pager Number(s): | |
| 5. Local Response Team (Fire Dept./Cooperatives): | |
| 6. Fire Marshall:<br>Evening Phone: | |
| 7. State Emergency Response Commission (SERC):<br>Evening Phone: | |
| 8. State Police: | |
| 9. Local Emergency Planning Committee (LEPC):<br>Evening Phone: | |
| 10. Local Water Supply System:<br>Evening Phone: | |
| 11. Weather Report: | |
| 12. Local Television/Radio Station for Evacuation Notification: | |
| 13. Hospitals: | |

## 2.1.2.2 Release Response Notification Form

| Reporting Party | Suspected responsible party |
|---|---|
| Reporter's Last Name: | Name: |
| First Name: | Phones :( ) |
| Middle Initial: | Company: |
| Position: | |
| Phone Numbers: | |
| Day ( ) | |
| Evening ( ) | |
| Company: | |
| Organization Type: | Organization Type: |
| Private citizen | Private citizen |
| Private enterprise | Private enterprise |
| Public utility | Public utility |
| Local government | Local government |
| State government | State government |
| Federal government | Federal government |
| Address: | City: |
| City: | State: |
| State: | Zip: |
| Zip: | |

Were Materials Discharged? _____ (Y/N) Confidential? _____ (Y/N)
Meeting Federal Obligations to Report? _____ (Y/N) Date Called: _____ Time Called: _____
Calling for Responsible Party? _____ (Y/N) Date Called: _____ Time Called: _____

| Incident Description |
|---|
| Source and/or Cause of Incident: |
| Date of Incident:<br>Time of Incident:           AM/PM<br>Incident Address/Location: |
| Nearest City:                          State:<br>County:                 Zip:<br>Distance from City:              Units of Measure:<br>Direction from City: |
| Section:            Township:                        Range:<br>Borough:<br>Container Type:          Storage Capacity:<br>Units of Measure:<br>Facility Latitude:         Degrees:          Minutes:<br>Seconds:<br>Facility Longitude:        Degrees:          Minutes:<br>Seconds: |

## Material

| CHRIS Code | Discharged quantity | Unit of measure | Where material was discharged | Quantify | Unit of Measure |
|---|---|---|---|---|---|
|  |  |  |  |  |  |

## Response Action

**Actions Taken to Correct, Control or Mitigate Incident:**

Impact

Number of Injuries: _____ Number of Deaths: _____

Were there Evacuations? _____ (Y/N) Number Evacuated: _____

Was there any Damage? _____ (Y/N) Damage in Dollars (approximate):
_____

Medium Affected: _____
Description: _____

More Information about Medium:
_____

Additional Information

Any information about the incident not recorded elsewhere in the report:



Caller Notification

EPA? _____ (Y/N) USCG? _____ (Y/N) State? ___ (Y/N) Other? ___
(Y/N) Describe: _____

## 2.1.3 Emergency Coordinator

At all times, there **must** be at least one employee either on the facility premises or on call (i.e., available to respond to an emergency by reaching the facility within a short period of time) with the responsibility for coordinating all emergency response measures. This emergency coordinator **must** be thoroughly familiar with all aspects of the facility's contingency plan, all operations and activities at the facility, the location and characteristics of waste handled, the location of all records within the facility, and the facility layout. In addition, this person **must** have the authority to commit the resources needed to carry out the contingency plan (40 CFR 264.55)).

## 2.1.4 Qualifications to be Emergency Coordinator

*(33 CFR 154.1026).*

• The qualified individual and alternate **must**:
(1) Be located in the United States;
(2) Speak fluent English;
(3) Be familiar with the implementation of the facility response plan; and
(4) Be trained in the responsibilities of the qualified individual under the response plan.

• The owner or operator *shall* provide each qualified individual and alternate qualified individual identified in the plan with a document designating them as a qualified individual and specifying their full authority to:
(1) Activate and engage in contracting with oil spill removal organization(s);
(2) Act as a liaison with the predesignated Federal On-Scene Coordinator (OSC); and
(3) Obligate funds required to carry out response activities.
• The owner or operator of a facility may designate an organization to fulfill the role of the qualified individual and the alternate qualified individual. The organization **must** then identify a qualified individual and at least one alternate qualified individual who meet the requirements of this section. The facility owner or operator is required to list in the response plan the organization, the person identified as the qualified individual, and the person or person(s) identified as the alternate qualified individual(s).
• The qualified individual is not responsible for—

(1) The adequacy of response plans prepared by the owner or operator; or (2) Contracting or obligating funds for response resources beyond the authority contained in their designation from the owner or operator of the facility.

• The liability of a qualified individual is considered to be in accordance with the provisions of 33 USC 1321(c)(4).

## 2.1.5 Emergency Procedure

Whenever there is an imminent or actual emergency situation, the emergency coordinator (or his designee when the emergency coordinator is on call) **must** immediately:

(1) Activate internal facility alarms or communication systems, where applicable, to notify all facility personnel; and

(2) Notify appropriate State or local agencies with designated response roles if their help is needed (40 CFR 264.56(a)(1)(2)).

If the emergency coordinator determines that the facility has had a release, fire, or explosion which could threaten human health, or the environment, outside the facility, he **must** report his findings as follows:

(1) If his assessment indicates that evacuation of local areas may be advisable, he **must** immediately notify appropriate local authorities. He **must** be available to help appropriate officials decide whether local areas should be evacuated; and

(2) He **must** immediately notify either the government official designated as the on-scene coordinator for that geographical area, (in the applicable regional contingency plan under part 1510 of this title) or the National Response Center (using their 24-hour toll free number 800/424-8802). The report **must** include:

(i)    Name and telephone number of reporter;

(ii)   Name and address of facility;

(iii)  Time and type of incident (e.g., release, fire);

(iv)   Name and quantity of material(s) involved, to the extent known;

(v)    The extent of injuries, if any; and

(vi)   The possible hazards to human health, or the environment, outside the facility (40 CFR 264.56(d)(1)(2)).

## 2.2 Establish of a response management structure

| RCRA (40 CFR part 264, Subpart D, 40 CFR Part 265, Subpart D, and 40 CFR 279.52 | EPA's Oil Pollution Prevention Regulation (40 CFR Part 112) | USCG-FRG (33 CFR Part 154) | DOT/RSPA-FRP (49 CFR part 194) | OSHA HAZWOPER (29 CFR 1910.120) |
|---|---|---|---|---|
| 264.37 265.37 279.52(a)(6) 264.52(c) 265.52(c) 279.52(b)(2)(iii) | 112.20(h)(1)(v) 112.20(h)(3)(v) F1.3.4 | 1035(a)(3)(iii) | 194.107(d)(1)(v) A-4 A-9 | (l)(2)(i),(ii) (p)(8)(ii)(A),(B) (q)(2)(i),(ii) (q)(3)(i) |

### 2.2.1 Response Activities

*(49 CFR 194, Appendix A-4):*

This section include the following

*   Responsibilities of, and actions to be taken by, operating personnel to initiate and supervise response actions pending the arrival of the qualified individual or other response resources identified in the response plan;

*   The qualified individual's responsibilities and authority, including notification of the response resources identified in the plan;

- Procedures for coordinating the actions of the operator or qualified individual with the action of the OSC responsible for monitoring or directing those actions;
- Oil spill response organizations available, through contract or other approved means, to respond to a worst case discharge to the maximum extent practicable; and
- For each organization identified under paragraph (d) of this section, a listing of:

(1) Equipment and supplies available; and
(2) Trained personnel necessary to continue operation of the equipment and staff the oil spill removal organization for the first 7 days of the response.

## 2.2.2 Response Zone Appendices.

*(49 CFR 194, Appendix A-9)*

Each response zone appendix provide the following information:

- The name and telephone number of the qualified individual;
- Notification procedures;
- Spill detection and mitigation procedures;
- Name, address, and telephone number of oil spill response organization;
- Response activities and response resources including—

(1) Equipment and supplies necessary to meet Sec. 194.115, and
(2) The trained personnel necessary to sustain operation of the equipment and to staff the oil spill removal organization and spill management team for the first 7 days of the response;
Names and telephone numbers of Federal, state and local agencies which the operator expects to assume pollution response responsibilities;

*The Worst Case Discharge Volume*

The method used to determine the worst case discharge volume, with calculations;

(i) A map that clearly shows—

(1) The location of the worst case discharge, and

(2) The distance between each line section in the response zone and—

(i) Each potentially affected public drinking water intake, lake, river, and stream within a radius of five miles of the line section, and

(ii) Each potentially affected environmentally sensitive area within a radius of one mile of the line section;

(j) A piping diagram and plan-profile drawing of each line section, which may be kept separate from the response plan if the location is identified; and

(k) For every oil transported by each pipeline in the response zone, emergency response data that—

(1) Include the name, description, physical and chemical characteristics, health and safety hazards, and initial spill-handling and firefighting methods; and

(2) Meet 29 CFR 1910.1200 or 49 CFR 172.602.

## 2.2.3 Pre-emergency planning and coordination with outside parties.

The plan **must** describe arrangements agreed to by local police departments, fire departments, hospitals, contractors, and State and local emergency response teams to coordinate emergency services, pursuant to Sec. 264.37 (40 CFR 264.52(c)).

The owner or operator **must** attempt to make the following arrangements, as appropriate for the type of waste handled at the facility and the potential need for the services of these organizations:

(1)   Arrangements to familiarize police, fire departments, and emergency response teams with the layout of the facility, properties of hazardous waste handled at the facility and associated hazards, places where facility personnel would normally be working, entrances to and roads inside the facility, and possible evacuation routes;

(2)   Where more than one police and fire department might respond to an emergency, agreements designating primary emergency authority to a specific police and a specific fire department, and agreement with any others to provide support to the primary emergency authority;

(3)   Agreement with State emergency response teams, emergency response contractors, and equipment suppliers; and

(4)   Arrangements to familiarize local hospitals with the properties of hazardous waste handled at the facility and the types of injuries or illnesses which could result from fires, explosions, or releases at the facility.

Where State or local authorities decline to enter into such arrangements, the owner or operator **must** document the refusal in the operating record (40 CFR 264.37).

## 2.2.4 Personnel roles, lines of authority, and communication.

Identification of personnel and their location, telephone numbers, and responsibilities for use of equipment in response activities on a 24-hour basis. The Emergency Response Personnel List *shall* be composed of all personnel employed by the facility whose duties involve responding to emergencies, including oil spills, even when they are not physically present at the site. An example of this type of person would be the Building Engineer-in-Charge or Plant Fire Chief.

Date of Last Update:_____

## EMERGENCY RESPONSE PERSONNEL
**Company Personnel**

| Name | Phone | Response Time | Responsibility during response action | Response training type/date |
|---|---|---|---|---|
| 1. | | | | |
| 2. | | | | |
| 3. | | | | |
| 4. | | | | |
| 5. | | | | |
| 6. | | | | |
| 7. | | | | |
| 8. | | | | |
| 9. | | | | |
| 10. | | | | |
| 11. | | | | |

[1] Phone number to be used when person is not on-site.

The Emergency Response Contractors (both primary and secondary) are retained by the facility. Any changes in contractor status **must** be reflected in updates to the ICP. Evidence of contracts with response contractors *shall* be included in this section.

## EMERGENCY RESPONSE CONTRACTORS

Date of Last Update:_____

| Contractor | Phone | Response Time | Contract Responsibility[1] |
|---|---|---|---|
| 1. | | | |
| | | | |
| 2. | | | |
| | | | |
| 3. | | | |
| | | | |
| 4. | | | |
| | | | |

# 2.3 Preliminary Assessment

| RCRA (40 CFR part 264, Subpart D, 40 CFR Part 265, Subpart D, and 40 CFR 279.52 | EPA's Oil Pollution Prevention Regulation (40 CFR Part 112) | USCG-FRG (33 CFR Part 154) | DOT/RSPA-FRP (49 CFR part 194) | OSHA Emergency Action Plans (29 CFR 1910.38(a)) and Process Safety (29 CFR 1910.119) | OSHA HAZWOPER (29 CFR 1910.120) |
|---|---|---|---|---|---|
| 264.56(b),(c)<br>265.56(b),(c)<br>279.52(b)(6)(ii),(iii) | 112.20(h)(3)(ix)<br>112.20(h)(4)<br>F1.4, F1.4.2 | 1035(b)(3)<br>1035(b)(4)(i) | 194.107(d)(1)(ii) | 38(a)(2)(i)<br>38(a)(2)(ii) | (l)(2)(i)<br>(l)(3)(vii)<br>(p)(8)(ii)(A)<br>(q)(2)(i)<br>(q)(3)(ii),(iii) |

## 2.3.1 Hazardous Evaluation

This section requires the facility owner or operator to examine the facility's operations closely and to predict where discharges could occur. Hazard evaluation is a widely used industry practice that allows facility owners or operators to develop a complete understanding of potential hazards and the response actions necessary to address these hazards. The Handbook of Chemical Hazard Analysis Procedures, prepared by the EPA, DOT, and the FEMA and the Hazardous Materials Emergency Planning Guide (NRT-1), prepared by the National Response Team are good references for conducting a hazard analysis. Hazard identification and evaluation will assist facility owners or operators in planning for potential discharges, thereby reducing the severity of discharge impacts that may occur in the future. The evaluation also may help the operator identify and correct potential sources of discharges. In addition, special hazards to workers and emergency response personnel's health and safety *shall* be evaluated, as well as the facility's oil spill history.

## 2.3.2 Hazard Identification

*Applicability.*

The owner or operator of a stationary source and other ICP facilities *shall* prepare a worst-case release and/or discharge scenario analysis, as well as a small and medium spill, as appropriate. A multi-level planning approach has been chosen because the response actions to a spill (i.e., necessary response equipment, products, and personnel) are dependent on the magnitude of the spill. Planning for lesser discharges is necessary because the nature of the response may be qualitatively different depending on the quantity of the discharge. The facility owner or operator *shall* discuss the potential direction of the spill pathway.

*Sec. 68.30 Defining offsite impacts—population..*

(a) The owner or operator *shall* estimate in the RMP the population within a circle with its center at the point of the release and a radius determined by the distance to the endpoint defined in Sec. 68.22(a).

(b) Population to be defined. Population *shall* include residential population. The presence of institutions (schools, hospitals, prisons), parks and recreational areas, and major commercial, office, and industrial buildings *shall* be noted in the RMP.

(c) Data sources acceptable. The owner or operator may use the most recent Census data, or other updated information, to estimate the population potentially affected.

(d) Level of accuracy. Population *shall* be estimated to two significant digits.

*Sec. 68.33 Defining offsite impacts—environment..*

(a) The owner or operator *shall* list in the RMP environmental receptors within a circle with its center at the point of the release and a radius determined by the distance to the endpoint defined in Sec. 68.22(a) of this part.

(b) Data sources acceptable. The owner or operator may rely on information provided on local U.S. Geological Survey maps or on any data source containing U.S.G.S. data to identify environmental receptors.

*68.36 Review and update.*

(a) The owner or operator *shall* review and update the offsite consequence analyses at least once every five years.

(b) If changes in processes, quantities stored or handled, or any other aspect of the stationary source might reasonably be expected to increase or decrease the distance to the endpoint by a factor of two or more, the owner or operator *shall* complete a revised analysis within six months of the change and submit a revised risk management plan as provided in Sec. 68.190.

## Toxic gas, Toxic liquid, and Flammables

*Risk assessments analysis parameters (40 CFR 68.22)*

- *Endpoints.* For analyses of offsite consequences, the following end-points *shall* be used:

    a. **Toxics.** The toxic endpoints provided in appendix A of this part.

    b. **Flammables.** The endpoints for flammables vary according to the scenarios studied:

    (i) **Explosion.** An overpressure of 1 psi.

    (ii) **Radiant heat/exposure time.** A radiant heat of 5 kw/m2 for 40 seconds.

    (iii) **Lower flammability limit.** A lower flammability limit as provided in NFPA documents or other generally recognized sources.

- *Wind speed/atmospheric stability class.* For the worst-case release analysis, the owner or operator *shall* use a wind speed of 1.5 meters per second and F atmospheric stability class. If the owner or operator can demonstrate that local meteorological data applicable to the stationary source show a higher minimum wind speed or less stable atmosphere at all times during the previous three years, these minimums may be used. For analysis of alternative scenarios, the owner or operator may use the typical meteorological conditions for the stationary source.

- *Ambient temperature/humidity.* For worst-case release analysis of a regulated toxic substance, the owner or operator *shall* use the highest daily maximum temperature in the previous three years and average humidity for the site, based on temperature/humidity data gathered at the stationary source or at a local meteorological station; an owner or operator using the RMP Offsite Consequence Analysis Guidance may use 25 deg.C and 50 percent humidity as values for these variables. For analysis of alternative scenarios, the owner or operator may use typical temperature/humidity data gathered at the stationary source or at a local meteorological station.

• *Height of release.* The worst-case release of a regulated toxic substance *shall* be analyzed assuming a ground level (0 feet) release. For an alternative scenario analysis of a regulated toxic substance, release height may be determined by the release scenario.

• *Surface roughness.* The owner or operator *shall* use either urban or rural topography, as appropriate. Urban means that there are many obstacles in the immediate area; obstacles include buildings or trees. Rural means there are no buildings in the immediate area and the terrain is generally flat and unobstructed.

• *Dense or neutrally buoyant gases.* The owner or operator *shall* ensure that tables or models used for dispersion analysis of regulated toxic substances appropriately account for gas density.

• *Temperature of released substance.* For worst case, liquids other than gases liquified by refrigeration only *shall* be considered to be released at the highest daily maximum temperature, based on data for the previous three years appropriate for the stationary source, or at process temperature, whichever is higher. For alternative scenarios, substances may be considered to be released at a process or ambient temperature that is appropriate for the scenario.

*Worst-case release scenario analysis (40 CRF 68.25)*

**a.** **The owner or operator shall analyze and report in the RMP:**

1. For Program 1 processes, one worst-case release scenario for each Program 1 process;
2. For Program 2 and 3 processes:

(i) One worst-case release scenario that is estimated to create the greatest distance in any direction to an endpoint provided in appendix A of this part resulting from an accidental release of regulated toxic substances from covered processes under worst-case conditions defined in Sec. 68.22;

(ii) One worst-case release scenario that is estimated to create the greatest distance in any direction to an endpoint defined in Sec. 68.22(a) resulting from an accidental release of regulated flammable substances from covered processes under worst-case conditions defined in Sec. 68.22; and

(iii) Additional worst-case release scenarios for a hazard class if a worst-case release from another covered process at the stationary source potentially affects public receptors different from those potentially affected by the worst-case release scenario developed under paragraphs (a)(2)(i) or (a)(2)(ii) of this section.

**(b)** **Determination of worst-case release quantity. The worst-case release quantity shall be the greater of the following:**

**(1)** For substances in a vessel, the greatest amount held in a single vessel, taking into account administrative controls that limit the maximum quantity; or

**(2)** For substances in pipes, the greatest amount in a pipe, taking into account administrative controls that limit the maximum quantity.

*Worst-case release scenario—toxic gasess.*

(1)   For regulated toxic substances that are normally gases at ambient temperature and handled as a gas or as a liquid under pressure, the owner or operator *shall* assume that the quantity in the vessel or pipe, as determined under paragraph (b) of this section, is released as a gas over 10 minutes. The release rate *shall* be assumed to be the total quantity divided by 10 unless passive mitigation systems are in place.

(2)   For gases handled as refrigerated liquids at ambient pressure:

(i) If the released substance is not contained by passive mitigation systems or if the contained pool would have a depth of 1 cm or less, the owner or operator *shall* assume that the substance is released as a gas in 10 minutes;

(ii) If the released substance is contained by passive mitigation systems in a pool with a depth greater than 1 cm, the owner or operator may assume that the quantity in the vessel or pipe, as determined under paragraph (b) of this section, is spilled instantaneously to form a liquid pool. The volatilization rate (release rate) *shall* be calculated at the boiling point of the substance and at the conditions specified in paragraph (d) of this section.

*Worst-case release scenario—toxic liquidss.*

(1)   For regulated toxic substances that are normally liquids at ambient temperature, the owner or operator *shall* assume that the quantity in the vessel or pipe, as determined under paragraph (b) of this section, is spilled instantaneously to form a liquid pool.

(i) The surface area of the pool *shall* be determined by assuming that the liquid spreads to 1 centimeter deep unless passive mitigation systems are in place that serve to contain the spill and limit the surface area. Where passive mitigation is in place, the surface area of the contained liquid *shall* be used to calculate the volatilization rate.

(ii) If the release would occur onto a surface that is not paved or smooth, the owner or operator may take into account the actual surface characteristics.

(2) The volatilization rate *shall* account for the highest daily maximum temperature occurring in the past three years, the temperature of the substance in the vessel, and the concentration of the substance if the liquid spilled is a mixture or solution.

(3) The rate of release to air *shall* be determined from the volatilization rate of the liquid pool. The owner or operator may use the methodology in the RMP Offsite Consequence Analysis Guidance or any other publicly available techniques that account for the modeling conditions and are recognized by industry as applicable as part of current practices. Proprietary models that account for the modeling conditions may be use provided the owner or operator allows the implementing agency access to the model and describes model features and differences from publicly available models to local emergency planners upon request.

*Worst-case release scenario—flammabless.*

The owner or operator *shall* assume that the quantity of the substance, as determined under paragraph (b) of this section, vaporizes resulting in a vapor cloud explosion. A yield factor of 10 percent of the available energy released in the explosion *shall* be used to determine the distance to the explosion endpoint if the model used is based on TNT-equivalent methods.

(f) **Parameters to be applied.** The owner or operator *shall* use the parameters defined in Sec. 68.22 to determine distance to the endpoints. The owner or operator may use the methodology provided in the RMP Offsite Consequence Analysis Guidance or any commercially or publicly available air dispersion modeling techniques, provided the techniques account for the modeling conditions and are recognized by industry as applicable as part of current practices. Proprietary models that account for the modeling conditions may be used provided the owner or operator allows the implementing agency access to the model and describes model features and differences from publicly available models to local emergency planners upon request.

**(g) Consideration of passive mitigation.** Passive mitigation systems may be considered for the analysis of worst case provided that the mitigation system is capable of withstanding the release event triggering the scenario and would still function as intended.

**(h) Factors in selecting a worst-case scenario.** Notwithstanding the provisions of paragraph (b) of this section, the owner or operator *shall* select as the worst case for flammable regulated substances or the worst case for regulated toxic substances, a scenario based on the following factors if such a scenario would result in a greater distance to an endpoint defined in Sec. 68.22(a) beyond the stationary source boundary than the scenario provided under paragraph (b) of this section:

(1) Smaller quantities handled at higher process temperature or pressure; and
(2) Proximity to the boundary of the stationary source.

*Alternative release scenario analysis (40 CFR 68.28)*

The number of scenarios. The owner or operator *shall* identify and analyze at least one alternative release scenario for each regulated toxic substance held in a covered process(es) and at least one alternative release scenario to represent all flammable substances held in covered processes.

Scenarios to consider. (1) For each scenario required under paragraph (a) of this section, the owner or operator *shall* select a scenario:

1.   That is more likely to occur than the worst-case release scenario under Sec. 68.25; and

2.  That will reach an endpoint offsite, unless no such scenario exists.

Release scenarios considered should include, but are not limited to, the following, where applicable:

Transfer hose releases due to splits or sudden hose uncoupling;

Process piping releases from failures at flanges, joints, welds, valves and valve seals, and drains or bleeds;

Process vessel or pump releases due to cracks, seal failure, or drain, bleed, or plug failure;

Vessel overfilling and spill, or overpressurization and venting through relief valves or rupture disks; and

Shipping container mishandling and breakage or puncturing leading to a spill.

*Parameters to be applied.*

The owner or operator *shall* use the appropriate parameters defined in Sec. 68.22 to determine distance to the endpoints. The owner or operator may use either the methodology provided in the RMP Offsite Consequence Analysis Guidance or any commercially or publicly available air dispersion modeling techniques, provided the techniques account for the specified modeling conditions and are recognized by industry as applicable as part of current practices. Proprietary models that account for the modeling conditions may be used provided the owner or operator allows the implementing agency access to the model and describes model features and differences from publicly available models to local emergency planners upon request.

*Consideration of mitigation.*

Active and passive mitigation systems may be considered provided they are capable of withstanding the event that triggered the release and would still be functional.

*Factors in selecting scenarios.*

The owner or operator *shall* consider the following in selecting alternative release scenarios:

(1) The five-year accident history provided in Sec. 68.42; and

(2) Failure scenarios identified under Sec. 68.50 or Sec. 68.67.

## EPA's Oil Pollution Prevention Regulation

*Preliminary Assessment (40 CFR 112, Appendix F 1.4, 1.4.2)*

The Tank and Surface Impoundment (SI) forms, or their equivalent, that are part of this section **must** be completed according to the directions below. ("Surface Impoundment" means a facility or part of a facility which is a natural topographic depression, man-made excavation, or diked area formed primarily of earthen materials (although it may be lined with man-made materials), which is designed to hold an accumulation of liquid wastes or wastes containing free liquids, and which is not an injection well or a seepage facility.) Similar worksheets, or their equivalent, **must** be developed for any other type of storage containers.

(1)   List each tank at the facility with a separate and distinct identifier. Begin aboveground tank identifiers with an "A" and belowground tank identifiers with a "B", or submit multiple sheets with the aboveground tanks and below ground tanks on separate sheets.

(2)   Use gallons for the maximum capacity of a tank; and use square feet for the area.

(3)   Using the appropriate identifiers and the following instructions, fill in the appropriate forms:

(a)     Tank or SI number—Using the aforementioned identifiers (A or B)) or multiple reporting sheets, identify each tank or SI at the facility that stores oil or hazardous materials.

(b)     Substance Stored—For each tank or SI identified, record thee material that is stored therein. If the tank or SI is used to store more than one material, list all of the stored materials.

(c)     Quantity Stored—For each material stored in each tank or SI,, report the average volume of material stored on any given day.

(d)     Tank Type or Surface Area/Year—For each tank, report the typee of tank (e.g., floating top), and the year the tank was originally installed. If the tank has been refabricated, the year that the latest refabrication was completed **must** be recorded in parentheses next to the year installed. For each SI, record the surface area of the impoundment and the year it went into service.

(e)     Maximum Capacity—Record the operational maximum capacity forr each tank and SI. If the maximum capacity varies with the season, record the upper and lower limits.

(f)     Failure/Cause—Record the cause and date of any tank or SII failure which has resulted in a loss of tank or SI contents.

(4)     Using the numbers from the tank and SI forms, label a schematic drawing of the facility. This drawing *shall* be identical to any schematic drawings included in the SPCC Plan.

(5)     Using knowledge of the facility and its operations, describe the following in writing:

(a)    The loading and unloading of transportation vehicles that risk the discharge of oil or release of hazardous substances during transport processes. These operations may include loading and unloading of trucks, railroad cars, or vessels. Estimate the volume of material involved in transfer operations, if the exact volume cannot be determined.

(b)    Day-to-day operations that may present a risk of discharging oil or releasing a hazardous substance. These activities include scheduled venting, piping repair or replacement, valve maintenance, transfer of tank contents from one tank to another, etc. (not including transportation-related activities). Estimate the volume of material involved in these operations, if the exact volume cannot be determined.

(c)    The secondary containment volume associated with each tank and/ or transfer point at the facility. The numbering scheme developed on the tables, or an equivalent system, **must** be used to identify each containment area. Capacities **must** be listed for each individual unit (tanks, slumps, drainage traps, and ponds), as well as the facility total.

(d)    Normal daily throughput for the facility and any effect on potential discharge volumes that a negative or positive change in that throughput may cause.

# HAZARD IDENTIFICATION TANKS[1]
**Date of Last Update:**_____

| Tank No. | Substance Stored (Oil and Hazardous Substance) | Quantity Stored (gallons) | Tank Type/Year | Maximum Capacity (gallons) | Failure/Cause |
|---|---|---|---|---|---|
| | | | | | |
| | | | | | |
| | | | | | |
| | | | | | |
| | | | | | |
| | | | | | |

[1] Tank = any container that stores oil or Hazardous Substance. Attach as many sheets as necessary.

# HAZARD IDENTIFICATION SURFACE IMPOUNDMENTS (Sis)
**Date of Last Update:** _____

| SI No. | Substance Stored (Oil and Hazardous Substance) | Quantity Stored (gallons) | Tank Type/Year | Maximum Capacity (gallons) | Failure /Cause |
|---|---|---|---|---|---|
| | | | | | |
| | | | | | |
| | | | | | |
| | | | | | |
| | | | | | |
| | | | | | |
| | | | | | |
| | | | | | |
| | | | | | |

*Small and Medium Discharges (40 CFR 112, Appendix F 1.5.1)*

To address multi-level planning requirements, the owner or operator **must** consider types of facility-specific spill scenarios that may contribute to a small or medium spill. The scenarios *shall* account for all the operations that take place at the facility, including but not limited to:

(1) Loading and unloading of surface transportation;

(2) Facility maintenance;

(3) Facility piping;

(4) Pumping stations and sumps;

(5) Oil storage tanks;

(6) Vehicle refueling; and

(7) Age and condition of facility and components.

The scenarios *shall* also consider factors that affect the response efforts required by the facility. These include but are not limited to:

(1) Size of the spill;

(2) Proximity to downgradient wells, waterways, and drinking water intakes;

(3) Proximity to fish and wildlife and sensitive environments;

(4) Likelihood that the discharge will travel offsite (i.e.,topography, drainage) ;

(5) Location of the material spilled (i.e., on a concrete pad or directly on the soil);

(6) Material discharged;

(7) Weather or aquatic conditions (i.e., river flow);

(8) Available remediation equipment;

(9) Probability of a chain reaction of failures; and

(10) Direction of spill pathway.

## *Worst Case Discharge (40 CFR 112, Appendix F 1.5.2)*

In this section, the owner or operator **must** identify the worst case discharge volume at the facility. Worksheets for production and non-production facility owners or operators to use when calculating worst case discharge are presented in Appendix D to this part. When planning for the worst case discharge response, all of the aforementioned factors listed in the small and medium discharge section of the response plan *shall* be addressed.

For onshore storage facilities and production facilities, permanently manifolded oil storage tanks are defined as tanks that are designed, installed, and/or operated in such a manner that the multiple tanks function as one storage unit (i.e., multiple tank volumes are equalized). In this section of the response plan, owners or operators **must** provide evidence that oil storage tanks with common piping or piping systems are not operated as one unit. If such evidence is provided and is acceptable to the RA, the worst case discharge volume *shall* be based on the combined oil storage capacity of all manifold tanks or the oil storage capacity of the largest single oil storage tank within the secondary containment area, whichever is greater. For permanently manifolded oil storage tanks that function as one storage unit, the worst case discharge *shall* be based on the combined oil storage capacity of all manifolded tanks or the oil storage capacity of the largest single tank within a secondary containment area, whichever is greater. For purposes of the worst case discharge calculation, permanently manifolded oil storage tanks that are separated by internal divisions for each tank are considered to be single tanks and individual manifolded tank volumes are not combined.

# 2.4 Establishment of objectives and priorities for response to the specific incident.

| RCRA (40 CFR part 264, Subpart D, 40 CFR Part 265, Subpart D, and 40 CFR 279.52 | EPA's Oil Pollution Prevention Regulation (40 CFR Part 112) | USCG-FRG (33 CFR Part 154) | DOT/RSPA-FRP (49 CFR part 194) | OSHA Emergency Action Plans (29 CFR 1910.38(a)) and Process Safety (29 CFR 1910.119) | OSHA HAZWOPER (29 CFR 1910.120) |
|---|---|---|---|---|---|
| 264.52(e) 265.52(e) 279.52(b)(2)(v) | 112.20(h)(1)(iv) 112.20(h)(1)(vii) 112.20(h)(3)(vi) 112.20(h)(3)(ix) F1.3.2 F1.7.1, F1.7.3 | 1035(a)(2) 1035(b)(3)(iv), (v) | 194.107(d)(1)(iii) 194.107(d)(1)(v) | 38(a)(4) 119(n) | (l)(2)(vi), (viii) (p)(8)(ii)(F), (H) (q)(2)(vi), (viii) (p)(8)(iv)(F) (q)(3)(ii),(iii),(iv) (vi),(vii) |

## RCRA

*(40 CFR 264.52(e))*

These objectives and priorities for response to the specific incident, include:

1) Immediate goals/tactical planning
2) Mitigating actions
3) Response resources

The plan **must** include a list of all emergency equipment at the facility (such as fire extinguishing systems, spill control equipment, communications and alarm systems (internal and external), and decontamination equipment), where this equipment is required. This list **must** be kept up to date. In addition, the plan **must** include the location and a physical description of each item on the list, and a brief outline of its capabilities.

## USCG-FRG

*Facility's spill mitigation procedures.*

(i) This subsection **must** describe the volume(s) and oil groups that would be involved in the—

(A) Average most probable discharge from the MTR facility;

(B) Maximum most probable discharge from the MTR facility;

(C) Worst case discharge from the MTR facility; and

(D) Where applicable, the worst case discharge from the non-transportation-related facility. This **must** be the same volume provided in the response plan for the non-transportation-related facility.

(ii) This subsection **must** contain prioritized procedures for facility personnel to mitigate or prevent any discharge or substantial threat of a discharge of oil resulting from operational activities associated with internal or external facility transfers including specific procedures to shut down affected operations. Facility personnel responsible for performing specified procedures to mitigate or prevent any discharge or potential discharge *shall* be identified by job title. A copy of these procedures *shall* be maintained at the facility operations center. These procedures **must** address actions to be taken by facility personnel in the event of a discharge, potential discharge, or emergency involving the following equipment and scenarios:

(A) Failure of manifold, mechanical loading arm, other transfer equipment, or hoses, as appropriate;

(B) Tank overfill;

(C) Tank failure;

(D) Piping rupture;

(E) Piping leak, both under pressure and not under pressure, if applicable;

(F) Explosion or fire; and

(G) Equipment failure (e.g. pumping system failure, relief valve failure, or other general equipment relevant to operational activities associated with internal or external facility transfers.)

(iii) This subsection **must** contain a listing of equipment and the responsibilities of facility personnel to mitigate an average most probable discharge.

*Facility's response activities.*

(i) This subsection **must** contain a description of the facility personnel's responsibilities to initiate a response and supervise response resources pending the arrival of the qualified individual.

(ii) This subsection **must** contain a description of the responsibilities and authority of the qualified individual and alternate as required in Sec. 154.1026.

(iii) This subsection **must** describe the organizational structure that will be used to manage the response actions. This structure **must** include the following functional areas.

(A) Command and control;

(B) Public information;

(C) Safety;

(D) Liaison with government agencies;

(E) Spill Operations;

(F) Planning;

(G) Logistics support; and

(H) Finance.

(iv) This subsection **must** identify the oil spill removal organizations and the spill management team to:

(A) Be capable of providing the following response resources:

(1) Equipment and supplies to meet the requirements of Secs. 154.1045, 154.1047 or subparts H or I of this part, as appropriate; and

(2) Trained personnel necessary to continue operation of the equipment and staff of the oil spill removal organization and spill management team for the first 7 days of the response.

(B) This section **must** include job descriptions for each spill management team member within the organizational structure described in paragraph (b)(3)(iii) of this section. These job descriptions should include the responsibilities and duties of each spill management team member in a response action.

(v) For mobile facilities that operate in more than one COTP zone, the plan **must** identify the oil spill removal organization and the spill management team in the applicable geographic-specific appendix. The oil spill removal organization(s) and the spill management team discussed in paragraph (b)(3)(iv)(A) of this section **must** be included for each COTP zone in which the facility will handle, store, or transport oil in bulk.

## 2.4.1 Plan Implementation

In this section, facility owners or operators **must** explain in detail how to implement the facility's emergency response plan by describing response actions to be carried out under the plan to ensure the safety of the facility and to mitigate or prevent discharges described in section 1.5 of the response plan. This section *shall* include the identification of response resources for small, medium, and worst case spills; disposal plans; and containment and drainage planning. A list of those personnel who would be involved in the cleanup *shall* be identified. Procedures that the facility will use, where appropriate or necessary, to update their plan after an oil spill event and the time frame to update the plan **must** be described.

## 2.4.2 Evacuation routes and procedures

The employer *shall* establish in the ICP the types of evacuation to be used in emergency circumstances 29 CFR 1910.38 (a)(4).

## 2.4.3 Emergency medical treatment and first aid

If a medical facility is not located in proximity to the workplace, the shall be a person or persons on-site with adequate first aid training. First-aid supplies approved by a consulting physician shall be available on-site. If there is the potential for corrosive materials on-site, suitable facilities shall be available for drenching of eyes and skin (29 CFR 1910.151).

## 2.4.4 Response Resources for Small, Medium, and Worst Case Spills

Once the spill scenarios have been identified in section 1.5 of the response plan, the facility owner or operator *shall* identify and describe implementation of the response actions. The facility owner or operator *shall* demonstrate accessibility to the proper response personnel and equipment to effectively respond to all of the identified spill scenarios. The determination and demonstration of adequate response capability are presented in Appendix E to this part. In addition, steps to expedite the cleanup of oil spills **must** be discussed. At a minimum, the following items **must** be addressed:

(1)   Emergency plans for spill response;
(2)   Additional response training;
(3)   Additional contracted help;
(4)   Access to additional response equipment/experts; and
(5)   Ability to implement the plan including response training and practice drills.

1.7.1.2A recommended form detailing immediate actions follows.

**Spill Response—Immediate Actionss**

| | |
|---|---|
| 1. Stop the product flow . . . . . . . | Act quickly to secure pumps, close valves, etc. |
| 2. Warn personnel . . . . . . . . . . | Enforce safety and security measures. |
| 3. Shut off ignition sources . . . . . | Motors, electrical circuits, open flames, etc. |
| 4. Initiate containment . . . . . . . | Around the tank and/or in the water with oil boom. |
| 5. Notify NRC . . . . . . . . . . . . | 1-800-424-8802 |
| 6. Notify OSC . . . . . . . . . . . . | |
| 7. Notify, as appropriate . . . . . . | |

Source: FOSS, Oil Spill Response—Emergency Procedures, Revised December 3, 1992.

## 2.4.5 Procedures for handling emergency response

The senior emergency response official responding to an emergency *shall* become the individual in charge of a site-specific Incident Command System (ICS). All emergency responders and their communications *shall* be coordinated and controlled through the individual in charge of the ICS assisted by the senior official present for each employer (29 CFR 1910.120(q)(3)(i)).

The individual in charge of the ICS *shall* identify, to the extent possible, all hazardous substances or conditions present and *shall* address as appropriate site analysis, use of engineering controls, maximum exposure limits, hazardous substance handling procedures, and use of any new technologies (29 CFR 1910.120(q)(3)(ii)).

Based on the hazardous substances and/or conditions present, the individual in charge of the ICS *shall* implement appropriate emergency operations, and assure that the personal protective equipment worn is appropriate for the hazards to be encountered. However, personal protective equipment *shall* meet, at a minimum, the criteria contained in 29 CFR 1910.156(e) when worn while performing fire fighting operations beyond the incipient stage for any incident. (29 CFR 1910.120(q)(3)(iii)).

Employees engaged in emergency response and exposed to hazardous substances presenting an inhalation hazard or potential inhalation hazard *shall* wear positive pressure self-contained breathing apparatus while engaged in emergency response, until such time that the individual in charge of the ICS determines through the use of air monitoring that a decreased level of respiratory protection will not result in hazardous exposure to employees (29 CFR 1910.120(q)(3)(iv)).

Back-up personnel *shall* stand by with equipment ready to provide assistance or rescue. Advance first aid support personnel, as a minimum, *shall* also stand by with medical equipment and transportation capability. (29 CFR 1910.120(q)(3)(vi)).

The individual in charge of the ICS *shall* designate a safety official, who is knowledgeable in the operations being implemented at the emergency response site, with specific responsibility to identify and evaluate hazards and to provide direction with respect to the safety of operations for the emergency at hand (29 CFR 1910.120(q)(3)(vii)).

## 2.4.6 Containment and Drainage Planning

A proper plan to contain and control a spill through drainage may limit the threat of harm to human health and the environment. This section *shall* describe how to contain and control a spill through drainage, including:

(1) The available volume of containment (use the information presented in section 1.4.1 of the response plan);

(2) The route of drainage from oil storage and transfer areas;

(3) The construction materials used in drainage troughs;

(4) The type and number of valves and separators used in the drainage system;

(5) Sump pump capacities;

(6) The containment capacity of weirs and booms that might be used and their location (see section 1.3.2 of this appendix); and

(7) Other cleanup materials.

In addition, facility owners or operators **must** meet the inspection and monitoring requirements for drainage contained in 40 CFR 112.7(e). A copy of the containment and drainage plans that are required in 40 CFR 112.7(e) may be inserted in this section, including any diagrams in those plans (40 CFR 112, Appendix F 1.7.3).

**Note: The general permit for stormwater drainage may contain additional requirements.**

## 2.4.7 Response Equipment List

A list of equipment that may be needed in response activities on land and navigable waters, including:

1) ☐ Transfer hoses and connection equipment

2) ☐ Portable pumps, skimmers, and ancillary equipment

| Type | Model | Year |
|------|-------|------|
|      |       |      |
|      |       |      |

Number:
Capacity:_____ gal./min.
Daily Effective Recovery Rate:
Storage Location(s):
Date Fuel Last Changed:

3) ☐ Boom—Operation Status

| Type | Model | Year |
|------|-------|------|
|      |       |      |
|      |       |      |

Number:
Size(length):_____ ft.
Containment Area:_____ sq. ft.
Storage Locations:

4) ☐ Chemicals Stored (Dispersants listed on EPA's NCP Product Schedule)

| Type | Amount | Date Purchased | Treatment Capacity | Storage Location |
|------|--------|----------------|--------------------|------------------|
|      |        |                |                    |                  |
|      |        |                |                    |                  |
|      |        |                |                    |                  |

Were appropriate procedures used to receive approval for use of dispersants in accordance with the NCP (40 CFR 300.910) and the Area Contingency Plan (ACP), Where applicable? _____ (Yes/No)

Name and State of On-Scene Coordinator (OSC) authorizing use: _____.

Date Authorized:_____.

5)   ☐   **Dispersant Dispensing Equipment-Operational Status**

| Type and Year | Capacity | Storage Location | Response Time (Minutes) |
|---------------|----------|------------------|-------------------------|
|               |          |                  |                         |
|               |          |                  |                         |
|               |          |                  |                         |
|               |          |                  |                         |

6)   ☐   **Sorbents—Operational Status:**_____

| Type and Year | Quantity | Storage Location |
|---------------|----------|------------------|
|               |          |                  |
|               |          |                  |
|               |          |                  |

7)   ☐   **Hand Tools—Operational Status:**_____

| Type and Year | Quantity | Storage Location |
|---------------|----------|------------------|
|               |          |                  |
|               |          |                  |
|               |          |                  |

8) ☐ Communication Equipment (include operating frequency and channel and/or cellular phone numbers)—Operation Status:

| Type and Year | Quantity | Storage Location/Number |
|---|---|---|
| | | |
| | | |
| | | |

9) ☐ Fire Fighting and Personnel Protective Equipment— Operational Status:_____

| Type and Year | Quantity | Storage Location |
|---|---|---|
| | | |
| | | |
| | | |

10) ☐ Other (e.g., Heavy Equipment, Boats and Motors)— Operational Status:_____

| Type and Year | Quantity | Storage Location |
|---|---|---|
| | | |
| | | |
| | | |

☐ Facilities available to transport and receive (i.e., oil, hazardous substances, hazardous waste, etc.) from a leaking (i.e., tank, pipeline, drum)

# 2.5 Implementation of tactical plan

| RCRA (40 CFR part 264, Subpart D, 40 CFR Part 265, Subpart D, and 40 CFR 279.52 | EPA's Oil Pollution Prevention Regulation (40 CFR Part 112) | USCG-FRG (33 CFR Part 154) | DOT/RSPA-FRP (49 CFR part 194) | OSHA Emergency Action Plans (29 CFR 1910.38(a)) and Process Safety (29 CFR 1910.119) | OSHA HAZWOPER (29 CFR 1910.120) |
|---|---|---|---|---|---|
| 264.52(e) 265.52(e) 279.52(b)(2)(v) | 112.20(h)(3)(ix) 112.20(h)(7) | 1035(b)(2)(iii) 1035(b)(3) 1035(b)(4)(iii) | 194.107(d)(1)(v) A-3 | 38(a)(2)(ii) | (l)(3)(vii) (p)(8)(iv)(F) (q)(3)(iii) |

## 2.5.1 Plan implementation.

The response plan *shall* describe:

(i) Response actions to be carried out by facility personnel or contracted personnel under the response plan to ensure the safety of the facility and to mitigate or prevent discharges described in paragraph (h)(5) of this section or the substantial threat of such discharges;

(ii) A description of the equipment to be used for each scenario;

(iii) Plans to dispose of contaminated cleanup materials; and

(iv) Measures to provide adequate containment and drainage of spilled oil (40 CFR 112(h)(7)).

**A description of the duties of the qualified individual identified in paragraph 40 CFR (h)(1) that include:**

(A) Activate internal alarms and hazard communication systems to notify all facility personnel;

(B)   Notify all response personnel, as needed;

(C)   Identify the character, exact source, amount, and extent of the release, as well as the other items needed for notification;

(D)   Notify and provide necessary information to the appropriate Federal, State, and local authorities with designated response roles, including the National Response Center, State Emergency Response Commission, and Local Emergency Planning Committee;

(E)   Assess the interaction of the spilled substance with water and/ or other substances stored at the facility and notify response personnel at the scene of that assessment;

(F)   Assess the possible hazards to human health and the environment due to the release. This assessment **must** consider both the direct and indirect effects of the release (i.e., the effects of any toxic, irritating, or asphyxiating gases that may be generated, or the effects of any hazardous surface water runoffs from water or chemical agents used to control fire and heat-induced explosion);

(G)   Assess and implement prompt removal actions to contain and remove the substance released;

(H)   Coordinate rescue and response actions as previously arranged with all response personnel;

(I)   Use authority to immediately access company funding to initiate cleanup activities; and

(J)   Direct cleanup activities until properly relieved of this responsibility (40 CFR 112.20(h)(3)(ix)).

The plan **must** include a list of all emergency equipment at the facility (such as fire extinguishing systems, spill control equipment, communications and alarm systems (internal and external), and decontamination equipment), where this equipment is required. This list **must** be kept up to date. In addition, the plan **must** include the location and a physical description of each item on the list, and a brief outline of its capabilities ( 40 CFR 279.52(b)(2)(v)).

# 2.6 Mobilization of Resources

| RCRA (40 CFR part 264, Subpart D, 40 CFR Part 265, Subpart D, and 40 CFR 279.52 | EPA's Oil Pollution Prevention Regulation (40 CFR Part 112) | USCG-FRG (33 CFR Part 154) | DOT/RSPA-FRP (49 CFR part 194) | OSHA HAZWOPER (29 CFR 1910.120) |
|---|---|---|---|---|
| 264.52(e) 265.52(e) 279.52(b)(2)(v) | 112.20(h)(7) F1.7.1 | 1035(b)(2)(iii) 1035(b)(3) 1035(b)(4)(iii) | 194.115 194.107(d)(1)(v) A-1 A-3 | (l)(2)(ix) (p)(8)(ii)(I) (q)(2)(ix) |

## RCRA

The plan **must** include a list of all emergency equipment at the facility (such as fire extinguishing systems, spill control equipment, communications and alarm systems (internal and external), and decontamination equipment), where this equipment is required. This list **must** be kept up to date. In addition, the plan **must** include the location and a physical description of each item on the list, and a brief outline of its capabilities.

## USCG-FRG

*Facility's response activities.*

(i) This subsection **must** contain a description of the facility personnel's responsibilities to initiate a response and supervise response resources pending the arrival of the qualified individual.

(ii) This subsection **must** contain a description of the responsibilities and authority of the qualified individual and alternate as required in Sec. 154.1026.

(iii) This subsection **must** describe the organizational structure that will be used to manage the response actions. This structure **must** include the following functional areas.

(A) Command and control;

(B) Public information;

(C) Safety;

(D) Liaison with government agencies;

(E) Spill Operations;

(F) Planning;

(G) Logistics support; and

(H) Finance.

(iv) This subsection **must** identify the oil spill removal organizations and the spill management team to:

(A) Be capable of providing the following response resources:

(1) Equipment and supplies to meet the requirements of Secs. 154.1045, 154.1047 or subparts H or I of this part, as appropriate; and

(2) Trained personnel necessary to continue operation of the equipment and staff of the oil spill removal organization and spill management team for the first 7 days of the response.

(B) This section **must** include job descriptions for each spill management team member within the organizational structure described in paragraph (b)(3)(iii) of this section. These job descriptions should include the responsibilities and duties of each spill management team member in a response action.

(v) For mobile facilities that operate in more than one COTP zone, the plan **must** identify the oil spill removal organization and the spill management team in the applicable geographic-specific appendix. The oil spill removal organization(s) and the spill management team discussed in paragraph (b)(3)(iv)(A) of this section **must** be included for each COTP zone in which the facility will handle, store, or transport oil in bulk.

*Fish and wildlife and sensitive environments.*

(i) This section of the plan must identify areas of economic importance and environmental sensitivity, as identified in the ACP, which are potentially impacted by a worst case discharge. ACPs are required under section 311(j)(4) of the FWPCA to identify fish and wildlife and sensitive environments. The applicable ACP *shall* be used to designate fish and wildlife and sensitive environments in the plan. Changes to the ACP regarding fish and wildlife and sensitive environments *shall* be included in the annual update of the response plan, when available.

(ii) For a worst case discharge from the facility, this section of the plan must—
(A) List all fish and wildlife and sensitive environments identified in the ACP which are potentially impacted by a discharge of persistent oils, non-persistent oils, or non-petroleum oils.
(B) Describe all the response actions that the facility anticipates taking to protest these fish and wildlife and sensitive environments.
(C) Contain a map or chart showing the location of those fish and wildlife and sensitive environments which are potentially impacted. The map or chart *shall* also depict each response action that the facility anticipates taking to protect these areas. A legend of activities **must** be included on the map page.

(iii) For a worst case discharge, this section **must** identify appropriate equipment and required personnel, available by contract or other approved means as described in Sec. 154.1028, to protect fish and wildlife and sensitive environments which fall within the distances calculated using the methods outlined in this paragraph as follows:

(A) Identify the appropriate equipment and required personnel to protect all fish and wildlife and sensitive environments in the ACP for the distances, as calculated in paragraph (b)(4)(iii)(B) of this section, that the persistent oils, non-persistent oils, or non-petroleum oils are likely to travel in the noted geographic area(s) and number of days listed in Table 2 of appendix C of this part;

(B) Calculate the distances required by paragraph (b)(4)(iii)(A) of this section by selecting one of the methods described in this paragraph;

(1) Distances may be calculated as follows:

(i) For persistent oils and non-petroleum oils discharged into non-tidal waters, the distance from the facility reached in 48 hours at maximum current.

(ii) For persistent and non-petroleum oils discharged into tidal waters, 15 miles from the facility down current during ebb tide and to the point of maximum tidal influence or 15 miles, whichever is less, during flood tide.

(iii) For non-persistent oils discharged into non-tidal waters, the distance from the facility reached in 24 hours at maximum current.

(iv) For non-persistent oils discharged into tidal waters, 5 miles from the facility down current during ebb tide and to the point of maximum tidal influence or 5 miles, whichever is less, during flood tide.

(2) A spill trajectory or model may be substituted for the distances calculated under paragraph (b)(4)(iii)(B)(l) of this section. The spill trajectory or model **must** be acceptable to the COTP.

(3) The procedures contained in the Environmental Protection's Agency's regulations on oil pollution prevention for non-transportation-related onshore facilities at 40 CFR part 112, appendix C, Attachment C-III may be substituted for the distances listed in non-tidal and tidal waters; and

(C) Based on historical information or a spill trajectory or model, the COTP may require the additional fish and wildlife and sensitive environments also be protected.

## DOT/RSPA-FRP

*Response resources*

(a) Each operator *shall* identify and ensure, by contract or other approved means, the resources necessary to remove, to the maximum extent practicable, a worst case discharge and to mitigate or prevent a substantial threat of a worst case discharge.

(b) An operator *shall* identify in the response plan the response resources which are available to respond within the time specified, after discovery of a worst case discharge, or to mitigate the substantial threat of such a discharge, as follows:

|  | Tier 1 | Tier 2 | Tier 3 |
|---|---|---|---|
| **High Volume Area** | 6 hrs | 30 hrs | 54 hrs |
| **All Other Areas** | 12 hrs | 36 hrs | 60 hrs |

*Response Plan: Section 1. Information Summary (49 CFR 194, Appendix A-1)*

Section 1 would include the following:

(a) For the core plan:

(1) The name and address of the operator; and

(2) For each response zone which contains one or more line sections that meet the criteria for determining significant and substantial harm as described in Sec. 194.103, a listing and description of the response zones, including county(s) and state(s).

(b) For each response zone appendix:

(1) The information summary for the core plan;

(2) The name and telephone number of the qualified individual, available on a 24-hour basis;

(3) A description of the response zone, including county(s) and state(s) in which a worst case discharge could cause substantial harm to the environment;

(4) A list of line sections contained in the response zone, identified by milepost or survey station number or other operator designation.

(5) The basis for the operator's determination of significant and substantial harm; and

(6) The type of oil and volume of the worst case discharge.

(c) The certification that the operator has obtained, through contract or other approved means, the necessary private personnel and equipment to respond, to the maximum extent practicable, to a worst case discharge or a substantial threat of such a discharge.

*Response Plan: Section 3. Spill Detection and On-Scene Spill Mitigation Procedures*

Section 3 would include the following:

(a) Methods of initial discharge detection;

(b) Procedures, listed in the order of priority, that personnel are required to follow in responding to a pipeline emergency to mitigate or prevent any discharge from the pipeline;

(c) A list of equipment that may be needed in response activities on land and navigable waters, including—

(1) Transfer hoses and connection equipment;

(2) Portable pumps and ancillary equipment; and

(3) Facilities available to transport and receive oil from a leaking pipeline;

(d) Identification of the availability, location, and contact telephone numbers to obtain equipment for response activities on a 24-hour basis; and

(e) Identification of personnel and their location, telephone numbers, and responsibilities for use of equipment in response activities on a 24-hour basis.

# Chapter 3

## Sustained Emergency Actions

### 3.0 Sustained actions

This section should address the transition of a response from the initial emergency stage to the sustained action stage where more prolonged mitigation and recovery actions progress under a response management structure. The NRT recognizes that most incidents are able to be handled by a few individuals without implementing an extensive response management system. This section of the core plan should be brief and rely heavily on references to specific annexes to the ICP.

| EPA's Oil Pollution Prevention Regulation (40 CFR Part 112) | USCG-FRG (33 CFR Part 154) | DOT/RSPA-FRP (49 CFR part 194) | OSHA Emergency Action Plans (29 CFR 1910.38(a)) and Process Safety (29 CFR 1910.119) | OSHA HAZWOPER (29 CFR 1910.120) | CAA RMP (40 CFR part 68) |
|---|---|---|---|---|---|
| 112.20(h)(7) | 1035(b)(3) | 194.107 (d)(1)(v) A-9 | 38(a)(2)(iii) | (l)(2)(ix) (p)(8)(ii)(J) (q)(2)(x) | 68.95(a)(1)(iii) |

## DOT/RSPA-FRP

*Response plan: Section 9. (49 CFR Part 194, Appendix A-9)*

Each response zone appendix would provide the following information:
(a) The name and telephone number of the qualified individual;
(b) Notification procedures;
(c) Spill detection and mitigation procedures;
(d) Name, address, and telephone number of oil spill response organization;
(e) Response activities and response resources including—
(1) Equipment and supplies necessary to meet Sec. 194.115, and
(2) The trained personnel necessary to sustain operation of the equipment and to staff the oil spill removal organization and spill management team for the first 7 days of the response;
(f) Names and telephone numbers of Federal, state and local agencies which the operator expects to assume pollution response responsibilities;
(g) The worst case discharge volume;
(h) The method used to determine the worst case discharge volume, with calculations;
(i) A map that clearly shows—
(1) The location of the worst case discharge, and
(2) The distance between each line section in the response zone and—
(i) Each potentially affected public drinking water intake, lake, river, and stream within a radius of 5 miles (8 kilometers) of the line section, and
(ii) Each potentially affected environmentally sensitive area within a radius of 1 mile (1.6 kilometer) of the line section;
(j) A piping diagram and plan-profile drawing of each line section, which may be kept separate from the response plan if the location is identified; and
(k) For every oil transported by each pipeline in the response zone, emergency response data that—

(1) Include the name, description, physical and chemical characteristics, health and safety hazards, and initial spill-handling and firefighting methods; and

(2) Meet 29 CFR 1910.1200 or 49 CFR 172.602.

# Chapter 4

## Termination of the Response

## 4.0 Termination and follow-up actions

This section should briefly address the development of a mechanism to ensure that the person in charge of mitigating the incident can, in coordination with the federal or state OSC as necessary, terminate the response. In the case of spills, certain regulations may become effective once the "emergency" is declared over. The section should describe how the orderly demobilization of response resources will occur. In addition, follow-up actions associated with termination of a response (e.g., accident investigation, response critique, plan review, written follow-up reports) should also be outlined in this section. Plan drafters may reference appropriate annexes to the ICP in this section of the core plan.

| RCRA (40 CFR part 264, Subpart D, 40 CFR Part 265, Subpart D, and 40 CFR 279.52 | EPA's Oil Pollution Prevention Regulation (40 CFR Part 112) | USCG-FRG (33 CFR Part 154) | OSHA HAZWOPER (29 CFR 1910.120) | CAA RMP (40 CFR part 68) |
|---|---|---|---|---|
| 264.56(i) 265.56(i) | 112.20(h)(7) | 1035(b)(3) | (l)(2)(ix) (p)(8)(ii)(I) (q)(2)(ix) | 68.95(a)(1)(iii) |

## RCRA

The emergency coordinator **must** ensure that, in the affected area(s) of the facility (40 CFR 264.56(h)):

(1) No waste that may be incompatible with the released material is treated, stored, or disposed of until cleanup procedures are completed; and

(2) All emergency equipment listed in the contingency plan is cleaned and fit for its intended use before operations are resumed.

(i) The owner or operator **must** notify the Regional Administrator, and appropriate State and local authorities, that the facility is in compliance with 40 CFR 264.56(h) before operations are resumed in the affected area(s) of the facility.

## USCG-FRG

*Facility's response activities.*

(i) This subsection **must** contain a description of the facility personnel's responsibilities to initiate a response and supervise response resources pending the arrival of the qualified individual.

(ii) This subsection **must** contain a description of the responsibilities and authority of the qualified individual and alternate as required in Sec. 154.1026.

(iii) This subsection **must** describe the organizational structure that will be used to manage the response actions. This structure **must** include the following functional areas.

(A) Command and control;

(B) Public information;

(C) Safety;

(D) Liaison with government agencies;

(E) Spill Operations;

(F) Planning;

(G) Logistics support; and

(H) Finance.

(iv) This subsection **must** identify the oil spill removal organizations and the spill management team to:

(A) Be capable of providing the following response resources:

(1) Equipment and supplies to meet the requirements of Secs. 154.1045, 154.1047 or subparts H or I of this part, as appropriate; and

(2) Trained personnel necessary to continue operation of the equipment and staff of the oil spill removal organization and spill management team for the first 7 days of the response.

(B) This section **must** include job descriptions for each spill management team member within the organizational structure described in paragraph (b)(3)(iii) of this section. These job descriptions should include the responsibilities and duties of each spill management team member in a response action.

(v) For mobile facilities that operate in more than one COTP zone, the plan **must** identify the oil spill removal organization and the spill management team in the applicable geographic-specific appendix. The oil spill removal organization(s) and the spill management team discussed in paragraph (b)(3)(iv)(A) of this section **must** be included for each COTP zone in which the facility will handle, store, or transport oil in bulk.

# Chapter 5

## Annexes

The annexes are designed to provide key supporting information for conducting an emergency response under the core plan as well as document compliance with regulatory requirements not addressed elsewhere in the ICP. Annexes are not meant to duplicate information that is already contained in the core plan, but to augment core plan information. The annexes should relate to the basic headings of the core plan. To accomplish this, the annexes should contain sections on facility information, notification, and a detailed description of response procedures under the response management system (i.e., command, operations, planning, logistics, and finance). The annexes should also address issues related to post accident investigation, incident history, written follow-up reports, training and exercises, plan critique and modification process, prevention, and regulatory compliance, as appropriate.

The ICP format contained in this guidance is based on the NIIMS ICS. If facility owners or operators choose to follow fundamental principles of the NIIMS ICS, then they may adopt NIIMS ICS by reference rather than having to describe the system in detail in the plan. The owner or operator should identify where NIIMS ICS documentation is kept at the facility and how it will be accessed if needed by the facility or requested by the reviewing agency. Regardless of the response management system used, the plan should include an organization chart, specific job descriptions,[3] a description of information flow ensuring liaison with the on-scene coordinator (OSC), and a description of how the selected response management system integrates with a Unified Command.[4] If a system other than NIIMS ICS is used, the plan should also identify how it differs from NIIMS or provide a detailed description of the system used.

The NRT anticipates that the use of linkages (i.e., references to other plans) when developing annexes will serve several purposes. Linkages will facilitate integration with other emergency plans within a facility (until such plans can be fully incorporated into the ICP) and with external plans, such as LEPC plans and Area Contingency Plans (ACPs). Linkages will also help ensure that the annexes do not become too cumbersome. The use of references to information contained in external plans does not relieve facilities from regulatory requirements to address certain elements in a facility-specific manner and to have information readily accessible to responders. When determining what information may be linked by reference and what needs to be contained in the ICP, response planners should carefully consider the time critical nature of the information. If instructions or procedures will be needed immediately during an incident response, they should be presented for ready access in the ICP. The following information would not normally be well-suited for reference to documents external to the ICP: core plan elements, facility and locality information (to allow for quick reference by responders on the layout of the facility and the surrounding environment and mitigating actions for the specific hazard(s) present), notification procedures, details of response management personnel's duties, and procedures for establishing the response management system. Although linkages provide the opportunity to utilize information developed by other organizations, facilities should note that many LEPC plans and ACPs may not currently possess sufficient detail to be of use in facility plans or the ICP. This information may need to be developed by the facility until detailed applicable information from broader plans is available.

In all cases, referenced materials **must** be readily available to anticipated plan users. Copies of documents that have been incorporated by reference need not be submitted unless it is required by regulation.

The appropriate sections of referenced documents that are unique to the facility, those that are not nationally recognized, those that are required by regulation, and those that could not reasonably be expected to be in the possession of the reviewing agency, should be provided when the plan is submitted for review and/or approval. Discretion should be used when submitting documents containing proprietary data. It is, however, necessary to identify in the ICP the specific section of the document being incorporated by reference, where the document is kept, and how it will be accessed if needed by the facility or requested by the reviewing agency. In addition, facility owners or operators are reminded to take note of submission requirements of specific regulations when determining what materials to provide an agency for review as it may not be necessary to submit all parts of an ICP to a particular agency.

[3]OPA 90 planning requirements for marine transfer facilities (33 CFR 154.1035) require job descriptions for each spill management team member regardless of the response management system employed by the facility.

[4]Under NIIMS ICS, the command module has traditionally been represented by a single incident commander (supported by a command staff) who directs efforts of and receives input from the four supporting functional areas (planning, logistics, operations, and finance). More recently, a Unified Command System as described in the National Oil and Hazardous Substances Pollution Contingency Plan (NCP) found at 40

CFR part 300 has been used for larger spill responses where the command module is comprised of representatives from the federal government (i.e., federal on-scene coordinator), state government (state on-scene coordinator), and the responsible party working in a cooperative manner. Unified Command allows all parties who have jurisdictional or functional responsibility for the incident to jointly develop a common set of incident objectives and strategies. Such coordination should be guided by procedures found in the NCP (see figure 1a at 40 CFR 300.105(e)(1)) and the applicable Area Contingency Plan.

## Annex 1.0 Facility and Locality Information

This annex should provide detailed information to responders on the layout of the facility and the surrounding environment. The use of maps and drawings to allow for quick reference is preferable to detailed written descriptions. These should contain information critical to the response such as the location of discharge sources, emergency shut-off valves and response equipment, and nearby environmentally and economically sensitive resources and human populations (e.g., nursing homes, hospitals, schools). The ACP and LEPC plan may provide specific information on sensitive environments and populations in the area. EPA Regional Offices, Coast Guard Marine Safety Offices, and LEPCs can provide information on the status of efforts to identify such resources. Plan holders may need to provide additional detail on sensitive areas near the facility. In addition, this annex should contain other facility information that is critical to response and should complement but not duplicate information contained in part 4 of the plan introduction section containing administrative information on the facility.

| EPA's Oil Pollution Prevention Regulation (40 CFR Part 112) | USCG-FRG (33 CFR Part 154) | DOT/RSPA-FRP (49 CFR part 194) |
|---|---|---|
| 112.20(h)(2) F1.2 F2.0 | 1035(a) 1035(e)(1) | 194.107(d)(1)(i) 194.113 194.113(b)(1) |

This section describes what is contained on the cover sheet. It also contains the introduction and content of the plan.

**Introduction and plan content.** This section of the plan **must** include facility and plan information as follows:

(1) The facility's name, street address, city, county, state, ZIP code, facility telephone number, and telefacsimile number, if so equipped. Include mailing address if different from street address.

(2) The facility's location described in a manner that could aid both a reviewer and a responder in locating the specific facility covered by the plan, such as, river mile or location from a known landmark that would appear on a map or chart.

(3) The name, address, and procedures for contacting the facility's owner or operator on a 24-hour basis.

(4) A table of contents.

(5) During the period that the submitted plan does not have to conform to the format contained in this subpart, a cross index, if appropriate (33 CFR 154.1035(a)).

Date of Last Update: _____

**Facility Information Form**

Facility Name:_____
Location (Street Address):_____
City: _____ State: _____ Zip: ____
County: _____ Phone Number: ( ) _____
    Latitude: _____ Degrees _____ Minutes _____ Seconds
    Longitude: _____ Degrees _____ Minutes _____ Seconds

Wellhead Protection Area:_____

Owner:_____
Owner Location (Street Address):_____
    (if different from Facility Address)
City: _____ State:_____ Zip:
County: _____ Phone Number: ( ) _____
Operator (if not Owner):_____

Qualified Individual(s): (attach additional sheets if more than one)
Name:_____
Position:_____ Work
Address:_____
Home Address:_____
Emergency Phone Number: ( )_____
Date of Oil Storage Start-up:_____
Current Operations:_____
_____
Date(s) and Type(s) of Substantial Expansion(s):_____
_____
(Attach additional sheets if necessary)

*Response Plan Cover Sheet*

A three-page form has been developed to be completed and submitted to the RA by owners or operators who are required to prepare and submit a facility-specific response plan. The cover sheet (Attachment F-1) **must** accompany the response plan to provide the Agency with basic information concerning the facility. This section will describe the Response Plan Cover Sheet and provide instructions for its completion.

*Applicability of Substantial Harm Criteria*

Using the flowchart provided in Attachment C-I to Appendix C to this part, mark the appropriate answer to each question. Explanations of referenced terms can be found in Appendix C to this part. If a comparable formula to the ones described in Attachment C-III to Appendix C to this part is used to calculate the planning distance, documentation of the reliability and analytical soundness of the formula **must** be attached to the response plan cover sheet.

*Attachment F-1—Response Plan Cover Sheett*

This cover sheet will provide EPA with basic information concerning the facility. It **must** accompany a submitted facility response plan. Explanations and detailed instructions can be found in Appendix F. Please type or write legibly in blue or black ink. Public reporting burden for the collection of this information is estimated to vary from 1 hour to 270 hours per response in the first year, with an average of 5 hours per response. This estimate includes time for reviewing instructions, searching existing data sources, gathering the data needed, and completing and reviewing the collection of information. Send comments regarding the burden estimate of this information, including suggestions for reducing this burden to: Chief, Information Policy Branch, PM-223, U.S. Environmental Protection Agency, 401 M St., SW., Washington, D.C. 20460; and to the Office of Information and Regulatory Affairs, Office of Management and Budget, Washington D.C. 20503.

**General Information**

Owner/Operator of Facility:

_____

Facility Name:_____
Facility Address (street address or route):

City, State, and U.S. Zip Code:

_____

Facility Phone No.:_____

Latitude (Degrees: North):

_____ degrees, minutes, seconds

Dun & Bradstreet Number: [1]
[1] These numbers may be obtained from public library resources.

_____

Largest Aboveground Oil Storage Tank Capacity (Gallons):

_____

Number of Aboveground Oil Storage Tanks:

_____

Longitude (Degrees: West):

_____

degrees, minutes, seconds_____

Standard Industrial Classification (SIC) Code: [1]_____

Maximum Oil Storage Capacity (Gallons):_____

Worst Case Oil Discharge Amount (Gallons):_____

Facility Distance to Navigable Water. Mark the appropriate line._____
0–1/4 mile _____ 1/4–1/2 mile _____ 1/2–1 mile _____ >1 mile _____

**Applicability of Substantial Harm Criteria**

Does the facility transfer oil over-water2 to or from vessels and does the facility have a total oil storage capacity greater than or equal to 42,000 gallons?

[2] Explanations of the above-referenced terms can be found in Appendix C to 40 CFR 112. If a comparable formula to the ones contained in 40 CFR 112, App. C Attachment C-III is used to establish the appropriate distance to fish and wildlife and sensitive environments or public drinking water intakes, documentation of the reliability and analytical soundness of the formula **must** be attached to this form.

Yes_____No_____

_____

Does the facility have a total oil storage capacity greater than or equal to 1 million gallons and, within any storage area, does the facility lack secondary containment2 that is sufficiently large to contain the capacity of the largest aboveground oil storage tank plus sufficient freeboard to allow for precipitation?

Yes_____

No_____

Does the facility have a total oil storage capacity greater than or equal to 1 million gallons and is the facility located at a distance2 (as calculated using the appropriate formula in 40 CFR 112, Appendix C or a comparable formula) such that a discharge from the facility could cause injury to fish and wildlife and sensitive environments?[3]

[3] For further description of fish and wildlife and sensitive environments, see Appendices I, II, and III to DOC/NOAA's "Guidance for Facility and Vessel Response Plans: Fish and Wildlife and Sensitive Environments" (see 40 CFR 112, Appendix E, section 10, for availability) and the applicable ACP.

Yes_____

No_____

Does the facility have a total oil storage capacity greater than or equal to 1 million gallons and is the facility located at a distance[2] (as calculated using the appropriate formula in Appendix C or a comparable formula) such that a discharge from the facility would shut down a public drinking water intake?[2]

Yes_____

No_____

Does the facility have a total oil storage capacity greater than or equal to 1 million gallons and has the facility experienced a reportable oil spill2 in an amount greater than or equal to 10,000 gallons within the last 5 years?

Yes_____

No_____

## Certification

I certify under penalty of law that I have personally examined and am familiar with the information submitted in this document, and that based on my inquiry of those individuals responsible for obtaining information, I believe that the submitted information is true, accurate, and complete.

Signature:_____

Name (Please type or print):_____

Title:_____

Date:_____

## A.1.1 Facility Maps and Facility Drawings

| RCRA (40 CFR part 264, Subpart D, 40 CFR Part 265, Subpart D, and 40 CFR 279.52 | EPA's Oil Pollution Prevention Regulation (40 CFR Part 112) | USCG-FRG (33 CFR Part 154) | DOT/RSPA-FRP (49 CFR part 194) |
|---|---|---|---|
| | 112.20(h)(1)(viii) 112.20(h)(9) F1.9 | 1035(e) | 194.113(b)(2) A-9 |

The facility-specific response plan *shall* include the following diagrams. Additional diagrams that would aid in the development of response plan sections may also be included.

Refer to the following regulations:

40 CFR 112.20, Appendix F1.9;
33 CFR 154.1035, and
49 CFR 194.113, Appendix A-9

**The Site Plan Diagram shall, as appropriate, include and identify:**

(A) the entire facility to scale;

(B) above and below ground bulk oil storage tanks;

(C) the contents and capacities of bulk oil storage tanks;

(D) the contents and capacity of drum oil storage areas;

(E) the contents and capacities of surface impoundments;

(F) process buildings;

(G) transfer areas;

(H) secondary containment systems (location and capacity);

(I) structures where hazardous materials are stored or handled, including materials stored and capacity of storage;

(J) location of communication and emergency response equipment;

(K) location of electrical equipment which contains oil; and

(L) for complexes only, the interface(s) (i.e., valve or component) between the portion of the facility regulated by EPA and the portion(s) regulated by other Agencies. In most cases, this interface is defined as the last valve inside secondary containment before piping leaves the secondary containment area to connect to the transportation-related portion of the facility (i.e., the structure used or intended to be used to transfer oil to or from a vessel or pipeline). In the absence of secondary containment, this interface is the valve manifold adjacent to the tank nearest the transfer structure as described above. The interface may be defined differently at a specific facility if agreed to by the RA and the appropriate Federal official.

**The Site Drainage Plan Diagram shall, as appropriate, include:**

(A) major sanitary and storm sewers, manholes, and drains;

(B) weirs and shut-off valves;

(C) surface water receiving streams;

(D) fire fighting water sources;

(E) other utilities;

(F) response personnel ingress and egress;

(G) response equipment transportation routes, and

(H) direction of spill flow from discharge points.

The Site Evacuation Plan Diagram shall, as appropriate, include:

(A) site plan diagram with evacuation route(s); and

(B) location of evacuation regrouping areas.

## A.1.2 Facility description/Layout

Identification of facility hazards and vulnerable resources and populations on and off the facility which may be impacted by an incident.

| EPA's Oil Pollution Prevention Regulation (40 CFR Part 112) | USCG-FRG (33 CFR Part 154) | DOT/R SPA-FRP (49 CFR part 194) | OSHA Emergency Action Plans (29 CFR 1910.38(a)) and Process Safety (29 CFR 1910.119) | OSHA HAZWOPER (29 CFR 1910.120) |
|---|---|---|---|---|
| F1.9 | 1035(b)(4) | A-9 | | (l)(3)(i)(A) (p)(8)(iv)(A)(1) |

# Annex 2.0 Notification

This annex should contain a general description of the facility's response management system as well as contain specific information necessary to guide or support the actions of each response management function (i.e., command, operations, planning, logistics, and finance) during a response.

The following chart summarizes who and what are involved in three typical emergency conditions. Information about the three response levels should be provided to special facilities (e.g., school districts, private schools, day care centers, hospitals, nursing homes, industries, detention centers).

| Response Level | Description | Contact |
|---|---|---|
| I. Potential Emergency Condition | An incident or threat of a release which can be controlled by the first response agencies and does not require evacuation of other than the involved structure or the immediate outdoor area. The incident is confined to a small area and does not pose an immediate threat to life or property. | Fire Department Emergency Medical Police Department Partial EOC Staff Public Information Office CHEMTREC National Response Center |
| II. Limited Emergency Condition | An incident involving a greater hazard or larger area which poses a potential threat to life or property and which may require a limited evacuation of the surrounding area. | All Agencies in Level I HAZMAT Teams EOC Staff Public Works Department Health Department Red Cross County Emergency Management Agency State Police Public Utilities |
| III. Full Emergency Condition | An incident involving a severe hazard or a large area which poses an extreme threat to life and property and will probably require a large scale evacuation; or an incident requiring the expertise or resources of county, State, Federal, or private agencies/ organizations. | All Level I and II Agencies plus the following as needed: Mutual Aid Fire, Police. Emergency Medical State Emergency Management Agency State Department of Environmental Resources Stage a Department of EPA, USCG, ATSDR FEMA, OSC/RRT |

| RCRA (40 CFR part 264, Subpart D, 40 CFR Part 265, Subpart D, and 40 CFR 279.52 | EPA's Oil Pollution Prevention Regulation (40 CFR Part 112) | DOT/RSPA-FRP (49 CFR part 194) | OSHA Emergency Action Plans (29 CFR 1910.38(a)) and Process Safety (29 CFR 1910.119) | OSHA HAZWOPER (29 CFR 1910.120) | CAA RMP (40 CFR part 68) |
|---|---|---|---|---|---|
| 264.52(d) 265.52(d) 279.52(b)(2)(iv) 264.56(a)(1),(2) 265.56(a)(1),(2) 279.52(b)(6)(i)(A),(B) 264.56(d)(1),(2) 265.56(d)(1),(2) 279.52(b)(6)(iv)(A),(B) | 112.20(h)(1)(ii) | 194.107(d)(1)(ii) A-2 | 38(a)(2)(v) 38(a)(2)(vi) 38(a)(3)(i) 38(a)(3)(ii) 165 | (l)(2)(ix) (p)(8)(ii)(I) (q)(2)(ix) | 68.95(a)(1)(i) |

This annex should detail the process of making people aware of an incident (i.e. who to call, when the call **must** be made, and what information/data to provide on the incident). The incident commander is responsible for ensuring that notifications are carried out in a timely manner but is not necessarily responsible for making notifications. ACPs, Regional Contingency Plans (RCPs), and LEPC plans should be consulted and referenced as a source of information on the roles and responsibilities of external parties that are to be contacted. This information is important to help company responders understand how external response officials fit into the picture. Call-down lists **must** be readily accessible to ensure rapid response. Notification lists provided in the core plan need not be duplicated here but need to be referenced.

## A.2.1 Internal

| EPA's Oil Pollution Prevention Regulation (40 CFR Part 112) | USCG-FRG (33 CFR Part 154) | DOT/RSPA-FRP (49 CFR part 194) | OSHA Emergency Action Plans (29 CFR 1910.38(a)) and Process Safety (29 CFR 1910.119) | OSHA HAZWOPER (29 CFR 1910.120) |
|---|---|---|---|---|
| 112.20(h)(3)(iii) F1.3.1 | 1035(b)(1)(i) 1035(b)(1)(ii) 1035(e)(2) | 194.107(d)(1)(iv) | 119(n) 165(b)(1) | (l)(2)(ix) (q)(2)(ix) (p)(8)(ii)(I) |

Section 2.1.2.1 of the core ICP describes the emergency notification phone list to contact the company's qualified individual and response team. There is also a release notification form in section 2.1.2.2 and at the end of this section.

## A.2.2 Community

| EPA's Oil Pollution Prevention Regulation (40 CFR Part 112) | USCG-FRG (33 CFR Part 154) | OSHA Emergency Action Plans (29 CFR 1910.38(a)) and Process Safety (29 CFR 1910.119) | OSHA HAZWOPER (29 CFR 1910.120) |
|---|---|---|---|
| 112.20(h)(3)(iii) 112.20(h)(3)(ix) F1.3.1 | 1035(b)(1)(i) 1035(b)(1)(ii) 1035(e)(2) | 119(n) | (l)(2)(i),(ii),(ix) (q)(2)(i),(ii),(ix) (p)(8)(ii),(A),(B),(I) |

Section 2.1.2.1 of the core ICP describes the emergency notification phone list to contact the community officials (i.e. Local Response teams such as the Fire Department, Local Emergency Planning Committee and Local Water Supply System). Also, telephone numbers for the Hospitals, Local Television/Radio Station for Evacuation, and Weather report.

## A.2.3 Federal and State Agency

| RCRA (40 CFR part 264, Subpart D, 40 CFR Part 265, Subpart D, and 40 CFR 279.52 | EPA's Oil Pollution Prevention Regulation (40 CFR Part 112) | USCG-FRG (33 CFR Part 154) | DOT/RSPA-FRP (49 CFR part 194) | OSHA Emergency Action Plans (29 CFR 1910.38(a)) and Process Safety (29 CFR 1910.119) | OSHA HAZWOPER (29 CFR 1910.120) | CAA RMP (40 CFR part 68) |
|---|---|---|---|---|---|---|
| | 112.20(h)(3)(iii) 112.20(h)(3)(ix) F1.3.1 | 1035(b)(1)(i) 1035(b)(1)(ii) 1035(e)(2) | 194.107(d)(1)(vi) | 119(n) | (l)(2)(i),(ii),(ix) (q)(2)(i),(ii),(ix) (p)(8)(ii),(A),(B),(I) | |

Section 2.1.2.1 of the core ICP describes the emergency notification phone list to contact the federal and state agencies (i.e. National Response Center, Federal On-Scene Coordinator, and State Emergency Response Commission). There is also a release notification form in section 2.1.2.2 and at the end of this section.

## Emergency Notification Phone List Whom to Notify

Date of Last Update:_____

**Reporter's Name:**
**Date:**
**Facility Name:**
**Owner Name:**
**Facility Identification Number:**
**Date and Time of Each NRC Notification:**

| Organization | Phone Number |
|---|---|
| 1.Qualified Individual:<br>Evening Phone: | |
| 2. National Response Center (NRC): | 1-800-424-8802 |
| 3. Company Response Team:<br>Evening Phone: | |
| 4. Federal On-Scene Coordinator (OSC) and/or Regional Response Center (RRC):<br>Evening Phone:<br>Pager Number(s): | |
| 5. Local Response Team (Fire Dept./Cooperatives): | |
| 6. Fire Mar*shall*:<br>Evening Phone: | |
| 7. State Emergency Response Commission (SERC):<br>Evening Phone: | |
| 8. State Police: | |
| 9. Local Emergency Planning Committee (LEPC):<br>Evening Phone: | |
| 10. Local Water Supply System:<br>Evening Phone: | |
| 11. Weather Report: | |
| 12. Local Television/Radio Station for Evacuation Notification: | |
| 13. Hospitals: | |

## Release Response Notification Form

| Reporting Party | Suspected responsible party |
|---|---|
| Reporter's Last Name: | Name: |
| First Name: | Phones:(  ) |
| Middle Initial: | Company: |
| Position: | |
| Phone Numbers: | |
| Day (  ) | |
| Evening (  ) | |
| Company: | |
| Organization Type: | Organization Type: |
| Private citizen | Private citizen |
| Private enterprise | Private enterprise |
| Public utility | Public utility |
| Local government | Local government |
| State government | State government |
| Federal government | Federal government |
| Address: | City: |
| City: | State: |
| State: | Zip: |
| Zip: | |

Were Materials Discharged? _____ (Y/N) Confidential? _____ (Y/N)
Meeting Federal Obligations to Report? _____ (Y/N) Date Called: _____ Time Called: _____
Calling for Responsible Party? _____ (Y/N) Date Called: _____ Time Called: _____

| Incident Description |
|---|
| Source and/or Cause of Incident: |
| |
| Date of Incident:<br>Time of Incident:　　　　　AM/PM<br>Incident Address/Location:<br><br>Nearest City:　　　　　　　State:<br>County:　　　　　Zip:<br>Distance from City:　　　　Units of Measure:<br>Direction from City:<br><br>Section:　　　Township:　　　　　Range:<br>Borough:<br>Container Type:　　　Storage Capacity:<br>Units of Measure:<br>Facility Latitude:　　　Degrees:　　　Minutes:<br>Seconds:<br>Facility Longitude:　　　Degrees:　　　Minutes:<br>Seconds: |

## Material

| CHRIS Code | Discharged quantity | Unit of measure | Where material was discharged | Quantity | Unit of Measure |
|---|---|---|---|---|---|
| | | | | | |

## Response Action

Actions Taken to Correct, Control or Mitigate Incident:

## Impact

Number of Injuries: _____ Number of Deaths: _____

Were there Evacuations? _____ (Y/N) Number Evacuated: _____

Was there any Damage? _____ (Y/N) Damage in Dollars (approximate): _____

Medium Affected:_____

Description:_____

More Information about Medium:

_____

## Additional Information

Any information about the incident not recorded elsewhere in the report:




## Caller Notification

EPA? _____ (Y/N) USCG? _____ (Y/N) State? ___ (Y/N)
Other?___ (Y/N) Describe: _____

_____

# Annex 3.0 Response Management Structure

This annex contains a general description of the facility's response management system as well as contains specific information necessary to guide management function (i.e. command, operations, planning, logistics, and finance) during a response.

| EPA's Oil Pollution Prevention Regulation (40 CFR Part 112) | USCG-FRG (33 CFR Part 154) | DOT/RSPA-FRP (49 CFR part 194) | OSHA HAZWOPER (29 CFR 1910.120) |
|---|---|---|---|
| 112.20(h)(1)(v) 112.20(h)(3)(v) F1.3.4 | 1035(b)(3)(iii) | 194.107(d)(1)(v) A-9 | (q)(3)(i) |

## A.3.1 General

If facility owners or operators choose to follow the fundamental principles of NIIMS ICS (see discussion of annexes above), then they may adopt NIIMS ICS by reference rather than having to describe the response management system in detail in the plan. In this section of Annex 3, planners should briefly address either 1) basic areas where their response management system is at variance with NIIMS ICS or 2) how the facility's organization fits into the NIIMS ICS structure. This may be accomplished through a simple organizational diagram.

If facility owners or operators choose not to adopt the fundamental principles of NIIMS ICS, this section should describe in detail the structure of the facility response management system. Regardless of the response management system used, this section of the annex should include the following information:

- Organizational chart;
- Specific job description for each position;
- A detailed description of information flow; and
- Description of the formation of a unified command within the response management system.

| RCRA (40 CFR part 264, Subpart D, 40 CFR Part 265, Subpart D, and 40 CFR 279.52 | USCG-FRG (33 CFR Part 154) | OSHA Emergency Action Plans (29 CFR 1910.38(a)) and Process Safety (29 CFR 1910.119) | OSHA HAZWOPER (29 CFR 1910.120) |
|---|---|---|---|
| 264.52 (c) 265.52(c) 279.52(b)(2)(iii) | 1035(b)(3)(iii) | 119(n) | (l)(2)(i),(ii),(ix) (q)(2)(i),(ii),(ix) (p)(8)(ii),(A),(B),(I) |

If facility owners or operators choose to follow the fundamental principles of NIIMS ICS (see discussion

The plan **must** describe arrangements agreed to by local police departments, fire departments, hospitals, contractors, and State and local emergency response teams to coordinate emergency services, pursuant to Sec. 264.37.

This subsection **must** describe the organizational structure that will be used to manage the response actions. This structure **must** include the following functional areas.
(A) Command and control;
(B) Public information;
(C) Safety;
(D) Liaison with government agencies;
(E) Spill Operations;

(F) Planning;

(G) Logistics support; and

(H) Finance.

## A.3.2 Command

List facility Incident Commander and Qualified Individual (if applicable) by name and/or title and provide information on their authorities and duties.

This section of Annex 3 should describe the command aspects of the response management system that will be used (i.e., reference NIIMS ICS or detail the facility's response management system). The location(s) of predesignated command posts should also be identified.

| EPA's Oil Pollution Prevention Regulation (40 CFR Part 112) | DOT/RSP A-FRP (49 CFR part 194) | OSHA Emergency Action Plans (29 CFR 1910.38(a)) and Process Safety (29 CFR 1910.119) | OSHA HAZWOPER (29 CFR 1910.120) |
|---|---|---|---|
| 112.20(h)(3)(iv) | | | (q)(3)(i) |

A description of information to pass to response personnel in the event of a reportable discharge.

### OSHA HAZWOPER

*Procedures for handling emergency response (29 CFR 1910.120(q)(3)(i))*

The senior emergency response official responding to an emergency *shall* become the individual in charge of a site-specific Incident Command System (ICS). All emergency responders and their communications *shall* be coordinated and controlled through the individual in charge of the ICS assisted by the senior official present for each employer.

Note to (q)(3)(i)—The "senior official" at an emergency response is the most senior official on the site who has the responsibility for controlling the operations at the site. Initially it is the senior officer on the first-due piece of responding emergency apparatus to arrive on the incident scene. As more senior officers arrive (i.e., battalion chief, fire chief, state law enforcement official, site coordinator, etc.) the position is passed up the line of authority which has been previously established (29 CFR 1910.120(q)(3)(i)).

## A.3.2.1 Facility incident commander and qualified individual

| RCRA (40 CFR part 264, Subpart D, 40 CFR Part 265, Subpart D, and 40 CFR 279.52 | EPA's Oil Pollution Prevention Regulation (40 CFR Part 112) | USCG-FRG (33 CFR Part 154) | DOT/RS PA-FRP (49 CFR part 194) | OSHA HAZWOPER (29 CFR 1910.120) |
|---|---|---|---|---|
| 264.55 265.55 279.52(b)(5) | 112.20(h)(1)(i)) F1.2.5 | 1026 | A-4 | (q)(3(i) |

## RCRA

*Emergency coordinator*

At all times, there **must** be at least one employee either on the facility premises or on call (i.e., available to respond to an emergency by reaching the facility within a short period of time) with the responsibility for coordinating all emergency response measures. This emergency coordinator **must** be thoroughly familiar with all aspects of the facility's contingency plan, all operations and activities at the facility, the location and characteristics of waste handled, the location of all records within the facility, and the facility layout. In addition, this person **must** have the authority to commit the resources needed to carry out the contingency plan.

[Comment: The emergency coordinator's responsibilities are more fully spelled out in Sec. 264.56. Applicable responsibilities for the emergency coordinator vary, depending on factors such as type and variety of waste(s) handled by the facility, and type and complexity of the facility.] (40 CFR 264.55)

*Qualified Individual*

Write the name of the qualified individual for the entire facility.

If more than one person is listed, each individual indicated in this section *shall* have full authority to implement the facility response plan. For each individual, list: name, position, home and work addresses (street addresses, not P.O. boxes), emergency phone number, and specific response training experience. (40 CFR 112.21 Appendix F1.2.5).

*Qualified Individual And Alternate Qualified Individual.*

(a) The response plan **must** identify a qualified individual and at least one alternate who meet the requirements of this section. The qualified individual or alternate **must** be available on a 24-hour basis and be able to arrive at the facility in a reasonable time.

(b) The qualified individual and alternate **must**:

(1) Be located in the United States;

(2) Speak fluent English;

(3) Be familiar with the implementation of the facility response plan; and

(4) Be trained in the responsibilities of the qualified individual under the response plan.

(c) The owner or operator *shall* provide each qualified individual and alternate qualified individual identified in the plan with a document designating them as a qualified individual and specifying their full authority to:

(1) Activate and engage in contracting with oil spill removal organization(s);

(2) Act as a liaison with the predesignated Federal On-Scene Coordinator (OSC); and

(3) Obligate funds required to carry out response activities.

(d) The owner or operator of a facility may designate an organization to fulfill the role of the qualified individual and the alternate qualified individual.

The organization **must** then identify a qualified individual and at least one alternate qualified individual who meet the requirements of this section. The facility owner or operator is required to list in the response plan the organization, the person identified as the qualified individual, and the person or person(s) identified as the alternate qualified individual(s).

(e) The qualified individual is not responsible for—
(1) The adequacy of response plans prepared by the owner or operator; or
(2) Contracting or obligating funds for response resources beyond the authority contained in their designation from the owner or operator of the facility.
(f) The liability of a qualified individual is considered to be in accordance with the provisions of 33 USC 1321(c)(4). (33 CFR 154.1026).

*Response Activities (49 CFR 194.121, Appendix A-4)*

(a) Responsibilities of, and actions to be taken by, operating personnel to initiate and supervise response actions pending the arrival of the qualified individual or other response resources identified in the response plan;
(b) The qualified individual's responsibilities and authority, including notification of the response resources identified in the plan;
(c) Procedures for coordinating the actions of the operator or qualified individual with the action of the OSC responsible for monitoring or directing those actions;
(d) Oil spill response organizations available, through contract or other approved means, to respond to a worst case discharge to the maximum extent practicable; and
(e) For each organization identified under paragraph (d) of this section, a listing of:
(1) Equipment and supplies available; and
(2) Trained personnel necessary to continue operation of the equipment and staff the oil spill removal organization for the first 7 days of the response.

## A.3.2.2 Information

This section of Annex 3 should address how the facility will disseminate information internally (i.e., to facility/response employees) and externally (i.e., to the public). For example, this section might address how the facility would interact with local officials to assist with public evacuation and other needs. Items to consider in developing this section include press release statement forms, plans for coordination with the news media, community relations plan, needs of special populations, and plans for families of employees.

| RCRA (40 CFR part 264, Subpart D, 40 CFR Part 265, Subpart D, and 40 CFR 279.52 | EPA's Oil Pollution Prevention Regulation (40 CFR Part 112) | USCG-FRG (33 CFR Part 154) | DOT/RSP A-FRP (49 CFR part 194) | OSHA Emergency Action Plans (29 CFR 1910.38(a)) and Process Safety (29 CFR 1910.119) | OSHA HAZWOPER (29 CFR 1910.120) |
|---|---|---|---|---|---|
| 264.56(a)(1),(2) 265.56(a)(1),(2) 279.52(b)(6)(i)(A), (B) | 112.20(h)(3)(iii) | 1035(b)(3)(iii) 1035(e)(4) | 194.107(d) (1)(v) A-2 | 38(a)(2)(vi) 38(a)(5)(iii) | (q)(3(i) |

## RCRA

*(40 CFR 264.56(a)(1)(2))*

Whenever there is an imminent or actual emergency situation, the emergency coordinator (or his designee when the emergency coordinator is on call) **must** immediately:

(1) Activate internal facility alarms or communication systems, where applicable, to notify all facility personnel; and

(2) Notify appropriate State or local agencies with designated response roles if their help is needed.

## EPA's Oil Pollution Prevention Regulation
*(40 CFR 112.20(h)(3)(iii)).*

The identity and the telephone number of individuals or organizations to be contacted in the event of a discharge so that immediate communications between the qualified individual identified in paragraph (h)(1) of this section and the appropriate Federal official and the persons providing response personnel and equipment can be ensured.

Names or regular job titles of persons or departments who can be contacted for further information or explanation of duties under the plan.

The employer *shall* review with each employee upon initial assignment those parts of the plan which the employee **must** know to protect the employee in the event of an emergency. The written plan *shall* be kept at the workplace and made available for employee review. For those employers with 10 or fewer employees the plan may be communicated orally to employees and the employer need not maintain a written plan. (29 CFR 1910.38(a)(2)(vi) and (a)(5)(iii))

*Notification Procedures (49 CFR 194.107(d)(1)(v) and A-2)*

(a) Notification requirements that apply in each area of operation of pipelines covered by the plan, including applicable State or local requirements;
(b) A checklist of notifications the operator or qualified individual is required to make under the response plan, listed in the order of priority;
(c) Names of persons (individuals or organizations) to be notified of a discharge, indicating whether notification is to be performed by operating personnel or other personnel;
(d) Procedures for notifying qualified individuals;
(e) The primary and secondary communication methods by which notifications can be made; and
(f) The information to be provided in the initial and each follow-up notification, including the following:

(1) Name of pipeline;

(2) Time of discharge;

(3) Location of discharge;

(4) Name of oil involved;

(5) Reason for discharge (e.g., material failure, excavation damage, corrosion);

(6) Estimated volume of oil discharged;

(7) Weather conditions on scene; and

(8) Actions taken or planned by persons on scene.

## A.3.2.3 Safety

This section of Annex 3 should include a process for ensuring the safety of responders. Facilities should reference responsibilities of the safety officer, federal/state requirements (e.g., HAZWOPER), and safety provisions of the ACP. Procedures for protecting facility personnel should be addressed (i.e., evacuation signals and routes, sheltering in place).

U.S. EPA Worker Protection Standards apply to employers of State and local governments whose employees are engaged in hazardous waste operations and emergency response. OSHA regulations apply directly to private and Federal employees and to those State and local government employees in States having OSHA-approved plans. OSHA and U.S. EPA worker protection standards (29 CFR 1910.120 and 40 CFR 11) implement Section 126 of SARA. U.S. EPA's worker protection regulations cover State and local government employees without OSHA-approved plans (reference 300.150 of the NCP).

An employer conducting a cleanup **must** comply with all the requirements in (b) through (o) of the OSHA standard. The requirements of (b) through (o) of the standard specify a minimum of 24 hours of off-site training. During emergency responses under 29 CFR 1910.120, the employer **must** comply with 1910.120 (q). If a post-emergency-response cleanup is done on plant property using plant or workplace employees, the employer **must** comply with the training requirements of 29 CFR 1910.38(a), 1910.134, 1910.120, and other appropriate training made necessary by the tasks they are expected to perform.

Based on experience with the standard (29 CFR 1910.120 [q][11][i]) during oil spills off the coasts of Texas, Alaska, and California, the hazards to employees vary widely in severity of potential injury or illness. For job duties and responsibilities with a low magnitude of risk, fewer than 24 hours of training may be appropriate for post-emergency cleanup workers. It is the expectation of OSHA that though the number of hours of training may vary, a minimum of 4 hours would be appropriate in most situations. Moreover, petroleum spills are unique in that many people who assist in the cleanup may not engage in this activity on a recurring basis. In addition, for maximum protection of the environment, petroleum spills dictate that cleanup **must** be completed as soon as possible (OSHA Instruction CPL 2-2.251). The DOL RRT representative is responsible for determining site-specific training requirements.

| RCRA (40 CFR part 264, Subpart D, 40 CFR Part 265, Subpart D, and 40 CFR 279.52 | EPA's Oil Pollution Prevention Regulation (40 CFR Part 112) | USCG-FRG (33 CFR Part 154) | OSHA Emergency Action Plans (29 CFR 1910.38(a)) and Process Safety (29 CFR 1910.119) | OSHA HAZWOPER (29 CFR 1910.120) |
|---|---|---|---|---|
| 264.52(f) 265.52(f) 279.52(b)(2) (vi) | 112.20(h)(1) (vi) 112.20(h)(3) (vii) 112.20(h)(3) (viii) F1.3.5 | 1035(b)(3) (iii) 1035(e)(5) | 38(a)(2)(i) 38(a)(2)(iii) 38(a)(2)(iv) 38(a)(4) | (1)(2)(iv),(vi) (p)(8)(ii)(D),(F) (q)(2)(iv),(vi) (q)(3)(vii),(viii) |

The plan **must** include an evacuation plan for facility personnel where there is a possibility that evacuation could be necessary. This plan **must** describe signal(s) to be used to begin evacuation, evacuation routes, and alternate evacuation routes (in cases where the primary routes could be blocked by releases of hazardous waste or fires).

The following are components of an evacuation plan:

- Safe distances and places of refuge.
- Evacuation routes and procedures.
- Emergency escape procedures and emergency escape route assignments;
- Procedures to account for all employees after emergency evacuation has been completed;
- Rescue and medical duties for those employees who are to perform them;
- Evacuation. The employer *shall* establish in the emergency action plan the types of evacuation to be used in emergency circumstances.

### A.3.2.3.1 Evacuation Plans

Based on the analysis of the facility, as discussed elsewhere in the plan, a facility-wide evacuation plan *shall* be developed. In addition, plans to evacuate parts of the facility that are at a high risk of expo-sure in the event of a discharge or other re-lease **must** be developed. Evacuation routes **must** be shown on a diagram of the facility. When developing evacuation plans, consideration **must** be given to the following factors, as appropriate:

(1) Location of stored materials;
(2) Hazard imposed by discharged material;
(3) Discharge flow direction;
(4) Prevailing wind direction and speed;
(5) Water currents, tides, or wave conditions (if applicable);
(6) Arrival route of emergency response personnel and response equipment;
(7) Evacuation routes;
(8) Alternative routes of evacuation;

(9) Transportation of injured personnel to nearest emergency medical facility;

(10) Location of alarm/notification systems;

(11) The need for a centralized check-in area for evacuation validation (roll call);

(12) Selection of a mitigation command center; and

(13) Location of shelter at the facility as an alternative to evacuation.

One resource that may be helpful to owners or operators in preparing this section of the response plan is The *Handbook of Chemical Hazard Analysis Procedures* by the Federal Emergency Management Agency (FEMA), Department of Transportation (DOT), and EPA. *The Handbook of Chemical Hazard Analysis Procedures* is available from:

FEMA , Publication Office, 500 C. Street, S.W., Washington, DC 20472, (202) 646–3484.

As specified in 40 CFR § 112.20(h)(1)(vi), the facility owner or operator **must** reference existing community evacuation plans, as appropriate. response actions necessary to address these hazards. *The Handbook of Chemical Hazard Analysis Procedures,* prepared by the EPA, DOT, and the FEMA and the *Hazardous Materials Emergency Planning Guide* (NRT–1), prepared by the National Response Team are good references for conducting a hazard analysis.

Hazard identification and evaluation will assist facility owners or operators in planning for potential discharges, thereby reducing the severity of discharge impacts that may occur in the future. The evaluation also may help the operator identify and correct potential sources of discharges. In addition, special hazards to workers and emergency response personnel's health and safety *shall* be evaluated, as well as the facility's oil spill history.

## A.3.2.4 Liaison

Response to a hazardous materials spill or release will involve many participants: police, firefighters, facility personnel, health personnel, and others. It is also possible to have more than one organization perform the same service; for example, local police, the county sheriff and deputies, as well as the highway patrol may respond to perform police functions. Because speed of response is so important, coordination is needed among the various agencies providing the same service. It is essential to identify (by title or position)the one individual responsible for each participating organization, and the one individual responsible for each major function and service. The plan might require that the responsible person establish an Incident Command System(ICS).

Work out, in advance, the following:
(1) Who will be in charge (lead organization)
(2) What will be the chain of command
(3) Who will activate the emergency operating center, if required
(4) Who will maintain the on-scene command post and keep it secure
(5) Who will have advisory roles (and what their precise roles are)
(6) Who will make the technical recommendations on response actions to the lead agency
(7) Who (if anyone) will have veto power
(8) Who is responsible for requesting assistance from outside the community

This chain of command should be clearly illustrated in a block diagram. Response action checklists are a way of condensing much useful information. They are helpful for a quick assessment of the response operation. If checklists are used, they should be prepared in sufficient detail to ensure that all crucial activities are included.

Planners should consider whether to have categories of response actions based on severity. The severity of an incident influences decisions on the level (or degree) of response to be made. This will determine how much equipment and how many personnel will be called, the extent of evacuation, and other factors.

| USCG-FRG (33 CFR Part 154) | DOT/RS PA-FRP (49 CFR part 194) | OSHA Emergency Action Plans (29 CFR 1910.38(a)) and Process Safety (29 CFR 1910.119) | OSHA HAZWOPER (29 CFR 1910.120) |
|---|---|---|---|
| 1035(b)(3)(iii) | | 38(a)(2)(vi) | (l)(2)(i),(ii) (p)(8)(ii)(A),(B) (q)(2)(i),(ii) |

**Pre-emergency planning.**
Personnel roles, lines of authority, and communication

Names or regular job titles of persons or departments who can be contacted for further information or explanation of duties under the plan.

## A.3.3 Operations

This section of Annex 3 should contain a discussion of specific operational procedures to respond to an incident. It is important to note that response operations are driven by the type of incident. That is, a response to an oil spill will differ markedly from a response to a release of a toxic gas to the air. Plan drafters should tailor response procedures to the particular hazards in place at the facility.

A facility with limited hazards may have relatively few procedures. A larger more complex facility with numerous hazards is likely to have a series of procedures

| USCG-FRG (33 CFR Part 154) | DOT/RSPA-FRP (49 CFR part 194) | OSHA Emergency Action Plans (29 CFR 1910.38(a)) and Process Safety (29 CFR 1910.119) | OSHA HAZWOPER (29 CFR 1910.120) |
|---|---|---|---|
| 1035(b)(3)(iii) | 194.107(d)(1)(v) | 38(a)(2)(i)-(iv) | (q)(3(iii), (v) |

*Response activities and response resources*

*Elements.*

The following elements, at a minimum, *shall* be included in the plan:
- Emergency escape procedures and emergency escape route assignments;
- Procedures to be followed by employees who remain to operate critical plant operations before they evacuate;
- Procedures to account for all employees after emergency evacuation has been completed;
- Rescue and medical duties for those employees who are to perform them;
- The preferred means of reporting fires and other emergencies; and
- Names or regular job titles of persons or departments who can be contacted for further information or explanation of duties under the plan.

Based on the hazardous substances and/or conditions present, the individual in charge of the ICS *shall* implement appropriate emergency operations, and assure that the personal protective equipment worn is appropriate for the hazards to be encountered. However, personal protective equipment *shall* meet, at a minimum, the criteria contained in 29 CFR 1910.156(e) when worn while performing fire fighting operations beyond the incipient stage for any incident.

The individual in charge of the ICS *shall* limit the number of emergency response personnel at the emergency site, in those areas of potential or actual exposure to incident or site hazards, to those who are actively performing emergency operations. However, operations in hazardous areas *shall* be performed using the buddy system in groups of two or more.

## A.3.3.1 Response Objectives

| USCG-FRG (33 CFR Part 154) | DOT/RSPA-FRP (49 CFR part 194) | OSHA Emergency Action Plans (29 CFR 1910.38(a)) and Process Safety (29 CFR 1910.119) | OSHA HAZWOPER (29 CFR 1910.120) |
|---|---|---|---|
| 1035(b)(2)(iii) 1035(b)(4)(iii) | | 38(a)(1) | (q)(3(iii), |

Based on the hazardous substances and/or conditions present, the individual in charge of the ICS *shall* implement appropriate emergency operations, and assure that the personal protective equipment worn is appropriate for the hazards to be encountered. However, personal protective equipment *shall* meet, at a minimum, the criteria contained in 29 CFR 1910.156(e) when worn while performing fire fighting operations beyond the incipient stage for any incident.

## A.3.3.2 Discharge or Release Control

| RCRA (40 CFR part 264, Subpart D, 40 CFR Part 265, Subpart D, and 40 CFR 279.52 | EPA's Oil Pollution Prevention Regulation (40 CFR Part 112) | USCG-FRG (33 CFR Part 154) | DOT/RSPA-FRP (49 CFR part 194) | OSHA Emergency Action Plans (29 CFR 1910.38(a)) and Process Safety (29 CFR 1910.119) |
|---|---|---|---|---|
| 264.56(e) 265.56(e) 279.52(b)(6)(v) | 112.20(h)(3)(i) 112.20(h)(7)(iv) 112.20(h)(1)(vii) | 1035(b)(2) 1035(b)(2)(iii) 1035(b)(4)(iii) | 194.107(d)(1)(v) A-3 | |

During an emergency, the emergency coordinator **must** take all reasonable measures necessary to ensure that fires, explosions, and releases do not occur, recur, or spread to other hazardous waste at the facility. These measures **must** include, where applicable, stopping processes and operations, collecting and containing release waste, and removing or isolating containers.

The identity of private personnel and equipment necessary to remove to the maximum extent practicable a worst case discharge and other discharges of oil described in paragraph (h)(5) of this section, and to mitigate or prevent a substantial threat of a worst case discharge (To identify response resources to meet the facility response plan requirements of this section, owners or operators *shall* follow Appendix E to this part or, where not appropriate, *shall* clearly demonstrate in the response plan why use of Appendix E of this part is not appropriate at the facility and make comparable arrangements for response resources);

Measures to provide adequate containment and drainage of discharged oil.

A description of immediate measures to secure the source of the discharge, and to provide adequate containment and drainage of discharged oil

*Response Plan: Section 3. Spill Detection and On-Scene Spill Mitigation Procedures*

a. Methods of initial discharge detection;
b. Procedures, listed in the order of priority, that personnel are required to follow in responding to a pipeline emergency to mitigate or prevent any discharge from the pipeline;
c. A list of equipment that may be needed in response activities on land and navigable waters, including—
(1) Transfer hoses and connection equipment;

(2) Portable pumps and ancillary equipment; and

(3) Facilities available to transport and receive oil from a leaking pipeline;

d. Identification of the availability, location, and contact telephone numbers to obtain equipment for response activities on a 24-hour basis; and

e. Identification of personnel and their location, telephone numbers, and responsibilities for use of equipment in response activities on a 24-hour basis.

*Facility's spill mitigation procedures.*

This subsection **must** describe the volume(s) and oil groups that would be involved in the—

(A) Average most probable discharge from the MTR facility;

(B) Maximum most probable discharge from the MTR facility;

(C) Worst case discharge from the MTR facility; and

(D) Where applicable, the worst case discharge from the non-transportation-related facility. This **must** be the same volume provided in the response plan for the non-transportation-related facility.

This subsection **must** contain prioritized procedures for facility personnel to mitigate or prevent any discharge or substantial threat of a discharge of oil resulting from operational activities associated with internal or external facility transfers including specific procedures to shut down affected operations. Facility personnel responsible for performing specified procedures to mitigate or prevent any discharge or potential discharge *shall* be identified by job title. A copy of these procedures *shall* be maintained at the facility operations center. These procedures **must** address actions to be taken by facility personnel in the event of a discharge, potential discharge, or emergency involving the following equipment and scenarios:

(A) Failure of manifold, mechanical loading arm, other transfer equipment, or hoses, as appropriate;

(B) Tank overfill;

(C) Tank failure;

(D) Piping rupture;

(E) Piping leak, both under pressure and not under pressure, if applicable;

(F) Explosion or fire; and

(G) Equipment failure (e.g. pumping system failure, relief valve failure, or other general equipment relevant to operational activities associated with internal or external facility transfers.)

This subsection **must** contain a listing of equipment and the responsibilities of facility personnel to mitigate an average most probable discharge.

## USCG-FRP

*(33 CFR part 154):*

For a worst case discharge, this section **must** identify appropriate equipment and required personnel, available by contract or other approved means as described in Sec. 154.1028, to protect fish and wildlife and sensitive environments which fall within the distances calculated using the methods outlined in this paragraph as follows:

(A) Identify the appropriate equipment and required personnel to protect all fish and wildlife and sensitive environments in the ACP for the distances, as calculated in paragraph (b)(4)(iii)(B) of this section, that the persistent oils, non-persistent oils, or non-petroleum oils are likely to travel in the noted geographic area(s) and number of days listed in Table 2 of appendix C of this part;

(B) Calculate the distances required by paragraph (b)(4)(iii)(A) of this section by selecting one of the methods described in this paragraph;

(1) Distances may be calculated as follows:

(i) For persistent oils and non-petroleum oils discharged into non-tidal waters, the distance from the facility reached in 48 hours at maximum current.

(ii) For persistent and non-petroleum oils discharged into tidal waters, 15 miles from the facility down current during ebb tide and to the point of maximum tidal influence or 15 miles, whichever is less, during flood tide. (iii) For non-persistent oils discharged into non-tidal waters, the distance from the facility reached in 24 hours at maximum current.

(iv) For non-persistent oils discharged into tidal waters, 5 miles from the facility down current during ebb tide and to the point of maximum tidal influence or 5 miles, whichever is less, during flood tide.

### A.3.3.3 Assessment/monitoring

| RCRA (40 CFR part 264, Subpart D, 40 CFR Part 265, Subpart D, and 40 CFR 279.52 | EPA's Oil Pollution Prevention Regulation (40 CFR Part 112) | USCG-FRG (33 CFR Part 154) | OSHA Emergency Action Plans (29 CFR 1910.38(a)) and Process Safety (29 CFR 1910.119) | OSHA HAZWOPER (29 CFR 1910.120) |
|---|---|---|---|---|
| 264.56(b),(c),(d),(f) 265.56(b),(c),(d),(f) 279.52(b)(6)(ii),(iii), (iv), (vi) | 112.20(h)(3)(ix) F1.7.1 | 1035(b)(3) 1035(b)(2)(iii) 1035(b)(4)(iii) | 38(a)(3)(ii) 38(a)(4) | (q)(3)(ii) |

### RCRA

*40 CFR 264.56(b),(c),(d),(f):*

Whenever there is a release, fire, or explosion, the emergency coordinator **must** immediately identify the character, exact source, amount, and a real extent of any released materials. He may do this by observation or review of facility records or manifests, and, if necessary, by chemical analysis.

Concurrently, the emergency coordinator **must** assess possible hazards to human health or the environment that may result from the release, fire, or explosion. This assessment **must** consider both direct and indirect effects of the release, fire, or explosion (e.g., the effects of any toxic, irritating, or asphyxiating gases that are generated, or the effects of any hazardous surface water run-off from water or chemical agents used to control fire and heat-induced explosions).

If the emergency coordinator determines that the facility has had a release, fire, or explosion which could threaten human health, or the environment, outside the facility, he **must** report his findings as follows:

(1) If his assessment indicates that evacuation of local areas may be advisable, he **must** immediately notify appropriate local authorities. He **must** be available to help appropriate officials decide whether local areas should be evacuated; and

(2) He **must** immediately notify either the government official designated as the on-scene coordinator for that geographical area, (in the applicable regional contingency plan under part 1510 of this title) or the National Response Center (using their 24-hour toll free number 800/424-8802). The report **must** include:
(i) Name and telephone number of reporter;
(ii) Name and address of facility;
(iii) Time and type of incident (e.g., release, fire);
(iv) Name and quantity of material(s) involved, to the extent known;
(v) The extent of injuries, if any; and
(vi) The possible hazards to human health, or the environment, outside the facility.

If the facility stops operations in response to a fire, explosion, or release, the emergency coordinator **must** monitor for leaks, pressure buildup, gas generation, or ruptures in valves, pipes, or other equipment, wherever this is appropriate.

## EPA's Oil Pollution Prevention Regulation

*40 CFR part 112.20(h)(3)(ix) and App. F 1.7.1:*

A description of the duties of the qualified individual identified in paragraph (h)(1) of this section, that include:

(A) Activate internal alarms and hazard communication systems to notify all facility personnel;

(B) Notify all response personnel, as needed;

(C) Identify the character, exact source, amount, and extent of the release, as well as the other items needed for notification;

(D) Notify and provide necessary information to the appropriate Federal, State, and local authorities with designated response roles, including the National Response Center, State Emergency Response Commission, and Local Emergency Planning Committee;

(E) Assess the interaction of the discharged substance with water and/or other substances stored at the facility and notify response personnel at the scene of that assessment;

(F) Assess the possible hazards to human health and the environment due to the release. This assessment **must** consider both the direct and indirect effects of the release (i.e., the effects of any toxic, irritating, or asphyxiating gases that may be generated, or the effects of any hazardous surface water runoffs from water or chemical agents used to control fire and heat-induced explosion);

(G) Assess and implement prompt removal actions to contain and remove the substance released;

(H) Coordinate rescue and response actions as previously arranged with all response personnel;

(I) Use authority to immediately access company funding to initiate cleanup activities; and

(J) Direct cleanup activities until properly relieved of this responsibility.

*1.7.1 Response Resources for Small, Medium, and Worst Case Discharges*

1.7.1.1 Once the discharge scenarios have been identified in section 1.5 of the response plan, the facility owner or operator *shall* identify and describe implementation of the response actions. The facility owner or operator *shall* demonstrate accessibility to the proper response personnel and equipment to effectively respond to all of the identified discharge scenarios. The determination and demonstration of adequate response capability are presented in Appendix E to this part. In addition, steps to expedite the clean-up of oil discharges **must** be discussed. At a minimum, the following items **must** be ad-dressed:

(1) Emergency plans for spill response;

(2) Additional response training;

(3) Additional contracted help;

(4) Access to additional response equipment/experts; and

(5) Ability to implement the plan including response training and practice drills.

1.7.1.2 A recommended form detailing immediate actions follows.

---

**OIL SPILL RESPONSE—IMMEDIATE ACTIONS**
1. Stop the product flow Act quickly to secure pumps, close valves, etc.
2. Warn personnel ......... Enforce safety and security measures.
3. Shut off ignition sources. Motors, electrical circuits, open flames, etc.
4. Initiate containment .... Around the tank and/or in the water with oil boom.
5. Notify NRC ................ 1–800–424–8802
6. Notify OSC
7. Notify, as appropriate
Source: FOSS, Oil Spill Response—Emergency Procedures, Revised December 3, 1992.

---

## A.3.3.4 Containment

| RCRA (40 CFR part 264, Subpart D, 40 CFR Part 265, Subpart D, and 40 CFR 279.52 | EPA's Oil Pollution Prevention Regulation (40 CFR Part 112) | USCG-FRG (33 CFR Part 154) | DOT/RSPA-FRP (49 CFR part 194) |
|---|---|---|---|
| 264.56(e) 265.56(e) 279.52(b)(6)(v) | 112.20(h)(3)(i) 112.20(h)(7)(iv) 112.20(h)(1)(vii) F1.7.3 | 1035(b)(2) 1035(b)(2)(iii) 1035(b)(4)(iii) | 194.107(d)(1)(v) |

*Containment and Drainage Planning (40 CFR Part 112, Appendix F 1.7.3)*

A proper plan to contain and control a discharge through drainage may limit the threat of harm to human health and the environment. This section *shall* describe how to contain and control a discharge through drainage, including:

(1) The available volume of containment (use the information presented in section 1.4.1 of the response plan);
(2) The route of drainage from oil storage and transfer areas;
(3) The construction materials used in drainage troughs;
(4) The type and number of valves and separators used in the drainage system;
(5) Sump pump capacities;
(6) The containment capacity of weirs and booms that might be used and their location (see section 1.3.2 of this appendix); and
(7) Other cleanup materials.

In addition, facility owners or operators **must** meet the inspection and monitoring requirements for drainage contained in 40 CFR 112.7(e). A copy of the containment and drainage plans that are required in 40 CFR

112.7(e) may be inserted in this section, including any diagrams in those plans.

**Note: The general permit for stormwater drainage may contain additional requirements.**

## A.3.3.5 Recovery

| RCRA (40 CFR part 264, Subpart D, 40 CFR Part 265, Subpart D, and 40 CFR 279.52 | EPA's Oil Pollution Prevention Regulation (40 CFR Part 112) | USCG-FRG (33 CFR Part 154) | DOT/RSPA-FRP (49 CFR part 194) |
|---|---|---|---|
| | 112.20(h)(3)(i) 112.20(h)(7)(iii) F1.7.2 | 1035(b)(2) 1035(b)(2)(iii) 1035(b)(4)(iii) | 194.107(d)(1)(v) |

**EPA's Oil Pollution Prevention Regulation**

*Disposal Plans (40 CFR 112, Appendix F 1.7.2)*

Facility owners or operators **must** describe how and where the facility intends to recover, reuse, decontaminate, or dispose of materials after a discharge has taken place. The appropriate permits required to transport or dispose of recovered materials according to local, State, and Federal requirements **must** be addressed. Materials that **must** be accounted for in the disposal plan, as appropriate, include:

(1) Recovered product;

(2) Contaminated soil;

(3) Contaminated equipment and materials, including drums, tank parts, valves, and shovels;

(4) Personnel protective equipment;

(5) Decontamination solutions;

(6) Adsorbents; and

(7) Spent chemicals.

These plans **must** be prepared in accordance with Federal (e.g., the Resource Conservation and Recovery Act [RCRA]), State, and local regulations, where applicable. A copy of the disposal plans from the facility's SPCC Plan may be inserted with this section, including any diagrams in those plans.

|   | Material | Disposal Facility | Location | RCRA Permit/Manifest |
|---|---|---|---|---|
| 1. | | | | |
| 2. | | | | |
| 3. | | | | |

## A.3.3.6 Decontamination

| RCRA (40 CFR part 264, Subpart D, 40 CFR Part 265, Subpart D, and 40 CFR 279.52 | EPA's Oil Pollution Prevention Regulation (40 CFR Part 112) | USCG-FRG (33 CFR Part 154) | DOT/RSPA-FRP (49 CFR part 194) | OSHA Emergency Action Plans (29 CFR 1910.38(a)) and Process Safety (29 CFR 1910.119) | OSHA HAZWOPER (29 CFR 1910.120) | CAA RMP (40 CFR part 68) |
|---|---|---|---|---|---|---|
| 264.56(h)(2) 265.56(h)(2) 279.52(b)(6)(viii)(B) | 112.20(h)(7)(iii) F1.7.2 | | 194.107(d)(1)(v) | | (k) (l)(2)(vii) (p)(8)(ii)(G) (q)(2)(vii) (q)(3)(ix) | |

*Decontamination (29 CFR 1910.120(k))*

(1) General. Procedures for all phases of decontamination *shall* be developed and implemented in accordance with this paragraph.

(2) Decontamination procedures. (i) A decontamination procedure *shall* be developed, communicated to employees and implemented before any employees or equipment may enter areas on site where potential for exposure to hazardous substances exists.

(ii) Standard operating procedures *shall* be developed to minimize employee contact with hazardous substances or with equipment that has contacted hazardous substances.

(iii) All employees leaving a contaminated area *shall* be appropriately decontaminated; all contaminated clothing and equipment leaving a contaminated area *shall* be appropriately disposed of or decontaminated.

(iv) Decontamination procedures *shall* be monitored by the site safety and health supervisor to determine their effectiveness. When such procedures are found to be ineffective, appropriate steps *shall* be taken to correct any deficiencies.

(3) Location. Decontamination *shall* be performed in geographical areas that will minimize the exposure of uncontaminated employees or equipment to contaminated employees or equipment.

(4) Equipment and solvents. All equipment and solvents used for decontamination *shall* be decontaminated or disposed of properly.

(5) Personal protective clothing and equipment. (i) Protective clothing and equipment *shall* be decontaminated, cleaned, laundered, maintained or replaced as needed to maintain their effectiveness.

(ii) Employees whose non-impermeable clothing becomes wetted with hazardous substances *shall* immediately remove that clothing and proceed to shower. The clothing *shall* be disposed of or decontaminated before it is removed from the work zone.

(6) Unauthorized employees. Unauthorized employees *shall* not remove protective clothing or equipment from change rooms.

(7) Commercial laundries or cleaning establishments. Commercial laundries or cleaning establishments that decontaminate protective clothing or equipment *shall* be informed of the potentially harmful effects of exposures to hazardous substances.

(8) Showers and change rooms. Where the decontamination procedure indicates a need for regular showers and change rooms outside of a contaminated area, they *shall* be provided and meet the requirements of 29 CFR 1910.141. If temperature conditions prevent the effective use of water, then other effective means for cleansing *shall* be provided and used.

## A.3.3.7 Non-responder Medical Needs

| USCG-FRG (33 CFR Part 154) | DOT/RS PA-FRP (49 CFR part 194) | OSHA Emergency Action Plans (29 CFR 1910.38(a)) and Process Safety (29 CFR 1910.119) | OSHA HAZWOPER (29 CFR 1910.120) | CAA RMP (40 CFR part 68) |
|---|---|---|---|---|
| 1035(e)(5) | | 38(a)(2)(iv) | (l)(2)(i), (ix) (p)(8)(ii)(H) (q)(2)(viii) | 68.95(a)(1)(ii) |

### A.3.3.7.1 Population Protective Actions

Protective actions for human populations are shelter in place, evacuation, or some combination of the two (e.g., evacuate the general population but shelter bedridden patients, jail populations). Guidance is currently being developed by FEMA in conjunction with other Federal Agencies on the decision-making process between evacuation and in-place sheltering. Until that guidance is available, it should be noted that if no decision is made, by default people will be sheltered in place, albeit not as effectively.

Documentation of proper first-aid and emergency medical treatment necessary to treat accidental human exposures.

### A.3.3.7.2 Treatment of Exposed Population

The first priority of response personnel is to assess the health and welfare of individuals involved in the emergency incident. Immediate medical attention is given to seriously injured persons; the hospital is alerted and transportation is requested as necessary.

(a) An initial survey of the area should be performed to determine radiologically contaminated areas and, if possible, to identify an uncontaminated area to which any injured persons can be removed.

(b) Contamination monitoring of all injured persons should be performed in the clean area and appropriate decontamination performed, if necessary.

(c) Seriously injured individuals who cannot be completely decontaminated should be wrapped in blankets to prevent the spread of contamination during transport.

(d) Individuals not completely decontaminated should be tagged to alert medical personnel to their contaminated status. Each tag should include the name of the individual, the injuries identified, the date and time of the incident, suspected contaminants, and the locations and levels of contamination.

(e) Provisions for appropriate testing should be made in all cases of suspected internal contamination of affected individuals or response personnel.

## A.3.3.8 Salvage Plans

| RCRA (40 CFR part 264, Subpart D, 40 CFR Part 265, Subpart D, and 40 CFR 279.52 | EPA's Oil Pollution Prevention Regulation (40 CFR Part 112) | USCG-FRG (33 CFR Part 154) | DOT/RSPA-FRP (49 CFR part 194) | OSHA Emergency Action Plans (29 CFR 1910.38(a)) and Process Safety (29 CFR 1910.119) | OSHA HAZWOPER (29 CFR 1910.120) | CAA RMP (40 CFR part 68) |
|---|---|---|---|---|---|---|
|  |  |  | 194.107(d)(1)(v) |  |  |  |

# A.3.4 Planning

| RCRA (40 CFR part 264, Subpart D, 40 CFR Part 265, Subpart D, and 40 CFR 279.52 | EPA's Oil Pollution Prevention Regulation (40 CFR Part 112) | USCG-FRG (33 CFR Part 154) | DOT/RSPA-FRP (49 CFR part 194) | OSHA Emergency Action Plans (29 CFR 1910.38(a)) and Process Safety (29 CFR 1910.119) | OSHA HAZWOPER (29 CFR 1910.120) | CAA RMP (40 CFR part 68) |
|---|---|---|---|---|---|---|
| | | | 194.107(a) 194.115 | 38(a)(1) 38(a)(4) | (l)(2)(i), (ix) (p)(8)(ii)(A),(I) q(1) (q)(2)(i),(ix) | |

## DOT/RSPA-FRP

Each response plan **must** plan for resources for responding, to the maximum extent practicable, to a worst case discharge, and to a substantial threat of such a discharge. (49 CFR 194.107(a))

*Response resources (49 CFR 194.115)*

(a) Each operator *shall* identify and ensure, by contract or other approved means, the resources necessary to remove, to the maximum extent practicable, a worst case discharge and to mitigate or prevent a substantial threat of a worst case discharge.

(b) An operator *shall* identify in the response plan the response resources which are available to respond within the time specified, after discovery of a worst case discharge, or to mitigate the substantial threat of such a discharge, as follows:

| | Tier 1 | Tier 2 | Tier 3 |
|---|---|---|---|
| **High Volume Area** | 6 hrs | 30 hrs | 54 hrs |
| **All Other Areas** | 12 hrs | 36 hrs | 60 hrs |

## A.3.4.1 Hazard Assessment

Hazard assessment, including facility hazards identification, vulnerability analysis, prioritization of potential risks.

This section of Annex 3 should present a detailed assessment of all potential hazards present at the facility, an analysis of vulnerable receptors (e.g., human populations, both workers and the general public, environmentally sensitive areas, and other facility-specific concerns) and a discussion of which risks deserve primary consideration during an incident. NRT-1 contains guidance on conducting a hazard analysis. Also, ACPs and LEPC plans may provide information on environmentally sensitive and economically important areas, human populations, and protection priorities. Plan drafters should address the full range of risks present at the facility. By covering actions necessary to respond to a range of incident types, plan holders can be prepared for small, operational discharges and large catastrophic releases. One approach that is required by certain regulations, such as the Clean Air Act (CAA) and OPA is to develop planning scenarios for certain types and sizes of releases (i.e., worst case discharge). Facilities may address such planning scenarios and associated calculations in this section of Annex 3 or as part of a separate annex depending on the size and complexity of the facility.

| EPA's Oil Pollution Prevention Regulation (40 CFR Part 112) | USCG-FRG (33 CFR Part 154) | DOT/RSPA-FRP (49 CFR part 194) | OSHA Emergency Action Plans (29 CFR 1910.38(a)) and Process Safety (29 CFR 1910.119) | OSHA HAZWOPER (29 CFR 1910.120) | CAA RMP (40 CFR part 68) |
|---|---|---|---|---|---|
| 112.20(h)(3)(ix) 112.20(h)(4) 112.20(h)(5) 112.20(h)(7)(ii) F1.4.1-F1.4.3 F1.5.1, F1.5.2 | 1029 1035(b)(4)(ii) | 194.105 194.113(b)(6) | 38(a)(4) | (l)(1)(ii)(C), (D) (p)(8)(iv)(A) (1),(F) (q)(3)(iii) | 68.20-36 68.50 68.67 |

## EPA's Oil Prevention Regulation

## (40 CFR 112, Appendix F1.4.1-1.4.3)

*Hazard Identification*

The Tank and Surface Impoundment (SI) forms, or their equivalent, that are part of this section **must** be completed according to the directions below. ("Surface Impoundment" means a facility or part of a facility which is a natural topographic depression, man-made excavation, or diked area formed primarily of earthen materials (although it may be lined with man-made materials), which is designed to hold an accumulation of liquid wastes or wastes containing free liquids, and which is not an injection well or a seepage facility.) Similar worksheets, or their equivalent, **must** be developed for any other type of storage containers.

(1) List each tank at the facility with a separate and distinct identifier. Begin aboveground tank identifiers with an "A" and below ground tank identifiers with a "B", or submit multiple sheets with the aboveground tanks and belowground tanks on separate sheets.

(2) Use gallons for the maximum capacity of a tank; and use square feet for the area.

(3) Using the appropriate identifiers and the following instructions, fill in the appropriate forms:

(a) Tank or SI number—Using the aforementioned identifiers (A or B) or multiple reporting sheets, identify each tank or SI at the facility that stores oil or hazardous materials..

(b) Substance Stored—For each tank or SI identified, record the material that is stored therein. If the tank or SI is used to store more than one material, list all of the stored materials..

(c) Quantity Stored—For each material stored in each tank or SI, report the average volume of material stored on any given day..

(d) Tank Type or Surface Area/Year—For each tank, report the type of tank (e.g., floating top), and the year the tank was originally installed. If the tank has been refabricated, the year that the latest refabrication was completed **must** be recorded in parentheses next to the year installed. For each SI, record the surface area of the impoundment and the year it went into service.

(e) Maximum Capacity—Record the operational maximum capacity for each tank and SI. If the maximum capacity varies with the season, record the upper and lower limits..

(f) Failure/Cause—Record the cause and date of any tank or SI failure which has resulted in a loss of tank or SI contents..

(4) Using the numbers from the tank and SI forms, label a schematic drawing of the facility. This drawing *shall* be identical to any schematic drawings included in the SPCC Plan.

(5) Using knowledge of the facility and its operations, describe the following in writing:

(a) The loading and unloading of transportation vehicles that risk the discharge of oil or release of hazardous substances during transport processes. These operations may include loading and unloading of trucks, railroad cars, or vessels. Estimate the volume of material involved in transfer operations, if the exact volume cannot be determined.

(b) Day-to-day operations that may present a risk of discharging oil or releasing a hazardous substance. These activities include scheduled venting, piping repair or replacement, valve maintenance, transfer of tank contents from one tank to another, etc. (not including transportation-related activities). Estimate the volume of material involved in these operations, if the exact volume cannot be determined.

(c) The secondary containment volume associated with each tank and/or transfer point at the facility. The numbering scheme developed on the tables, or an equivalent system, **must** be used to identify each containment area. Capacities **must** be listed for each individual unit (tanks, slumps, drainage traps, and ponds), as well as the facility total.

(d) Normal daily throughput for the facility and any effect on potential discharge volumes that a negative or positive change in that throughput may cause.

### Hazard Identification Tanks[1]

Date of Last Update: _____

| Tank No. | Substance Stored (Oil and Hazardous Substance) | Quantity Stored (gallons) | Tank Type/ Year | Maximum Capacity(gallons) | Failure/Cause |
|---|---|---|---|---|---|
| | | | | | |
| | | | | | |
| | | | | | |

[1] Tank = any container that stores oil.
Attach as many sheets as necessary.

Hazard Identification Surface Impoundments (SIs)
Date of Last Update:

| SI No. | Substance Stored (Oil and Hazardous Substance) | Quantity Stored (gallons) | Tank Type/Year | Maximum Capacity(gallons) | Failure/Cause |
|---|---|---|---|---|---|
| | | | | | |
| | | | | | |
| | | | | | |

Attach as many sheets as necessary.

*Vulnerability Analysis*

The vulnerability analysis *shall* address the potential effects (i.e., to human health, property, or the environment) of an oil discharge. Attachment C-III to Appendix C to this part provides a method that owners or operators *shall* use to determine appropriate distances from the facility to fish and wildlife and sensitive environments.

Owners or operators can use a comparable formula that is considered acceptable by the RA. If a comparable formula is used, documentation of the reliability and analytical soundness of the formula **must** be attached to the response plan cover sheet. This analysis **must** be prepared for each facility and, as appropriate, **must** discuss the vulnerability of:

(1) Water intakes (drinking, cooling, or other);
(2) Schools;
(3) Medical facilities;
(4) Residential areas;
(5) Businesses;
(6) Wetlands or other sensitive environments; 2
(7) Fish and wildlife;
(8) Lakes and streams;
(9) Endangered flora and fauna;
(10) Recreational areas;

(11) Transportation routes (air, land, and water);
(12) Utilities; and
(13) Other areas of economic importance (e.g., beaches, marinas) including terrestrially sensitive environments, aquatic environments, and unique habitats.

2 Refer to the DOC/NOAA "Guidance for Facility and Vessel Response Plans: Fish and Wildlife and Sensitive Environments" (See appendix E to this part, section 13, for availability).

*Analysis of the Potential for an Oil Discharge*

Each owner or operator *shall* analyze the probability of a discharge occurring at the facility. This analysis *shall* incorporate factors such as oil spill history, horizontal range of a potential discharge, and vulnerability to natural disaster, and *shall*, as appropriate, incorporate other factors such as tank age. This analysis will provide information for developing discharge scenarios for a worst case discharge and small and medium discharges and aid in the development of techniques to reduce the size and frequency of discharges. The owner or operator may need to research the age of the tanks and the oil spill history at the facility.

*Discharge Scenarios*

In this section, the owner or operator is required to provide a description of the facility's worst case discharge, as well as a small and medium discharge, as appropriate. A multi-level planning approach has been chosen because the response actions to a discharge (i.e., necessary response equipment, products, and personnel) are dependent on the magnitude of the discharge. Planning for lesser discharges is necessary because the nature of the response may be qualitatively different depending on the quantity of the discharge. The facility owner or operator *shall* discuss the potential direction of the discharge pathway.

*Small and Medium Discharges*

To address multi-level planning requirements, the owner or operator **must** consider types of facility-specific discharge scenarios that may contribute to a small or medium discharge. The scenarios *shall* account for all the operations that take place at the facility, including but not limited to:
(1) Loading and unloading of surface transportation;
(2) Facility maintenance;
(3) Facility piping;
(4) Pumping stations and sumps;
(5) Oil storage tanks;
(6) Vehicle refueling; and
(7) Age and condition of facility and components.
The scenarios *shall* also consider factors that affect the response efforts required by the facility. These include but are not limited to:

(1) Size of the discharge;
(2) Proximity to downgradient wells, waterways, and drinking water intakes;
(3) Proximity to fish and wildlife and sensitive environments;
(4) Likelihood that the discharge will travel offsite (i.e., topography, drainage);
(5) Location of the material discharged (i.e., on a concrete pad or directly on the soil);
(6) Material discharged;
(7) Weather or aquatic conditions (i.e., river flow);
(8) Available remediation equipment;
(9) Probability of a chain reaction of failures; and
(10) Direction of discharge pathway.

*Worst Case Discharge*

In this section, the owner or operator **must** identify the worst case discharge volume at the facility. Worksheets for production and non-production facility owners or operators to use when calculating worst case discharge are presented in Appendix D to this part. When planning for the worst case discharge response, all of the aforementioned factors listed in the small and medium discharge section of the response plan *shall* be addressed.

For onshore storage facilities and production facilities, permanently manifolded oil storage tanks are defined as tanks that are designed, installed, and/or operated in such a manner that the multiple tanks function as one storage unit (i.e., multiple tank volumes are equalized). In this section of the response plan, owners or operators **must** provide evidence that oil storage tanks with common piping or piping systems are not operated as one unit. If such evidence is provided and is acceptable to the RA, the worst case discharge volume *shall* be based on the combined oil storage capacity of all manifold tanks or the oil storage capacity of the largest single oil storage tank within the secondary containment area, whichever is greater. For permanently manifolded oil storage tanks that function as one storage unit, the worst case discharge *shall* be based on the combined oil storage capacity of all manifolded tanks or the oil storage capacity of the largest single tank within a secondary containment area, whichever is greater. For purposes of the worst case discharge calculation, permanently manifolded oil storage tanks that are separated by internal divisions for each tank are considered to be single tanks and individual manifolded tank volumes are not combined.

*Worst case discharge USCG-FRP (33 CFR 154.1029)*

(a) The response plan **must** use the appropriate criteria in this section to develop the worst case discharge.
(b) For the MTR segment of a facility, not less than—

(1) Where applicable, the loss of the entire capacity of all in-line and break out tank(s) needed for the continuous operation of the pipelines used for the purposes of handling or transporting oil, in bulk, to or from a vessel regardless of the presence of secondary containment; plus

(2) The discharge from all piping carrying oil between the marine transfer manifold and the non-transportation-related portion of the facility. The discharge from each pipe is calculated as follows: The maximum time to discover the release from the pipe in hours, plus the maximum time to shut down flow from the pipe in hours (based on historic discharge data or the best estimate in the absence of historic discharge data for the facility) multiplied by the maximum flow rate expressed in barrels per hour (based on the maximum relief valve setting or maximum system pressure when relief valves are not provided) plus the total line drainage volume expressed in barrels for the pipe between the marine manifold and the non-transportation-related portion of the facility; and

(c) For a mobile facility it means the loss of the entire contents of the container in which the oil is stored or transported.

*Worst case discharge (49 CFR 194.105)*

(a) Each operator *shall* determine the worst case discharge for each of its response zones and provide the methodology, including calculations, used to arrive at the volume.

(b) The worst case discharge is the largest volume, in barrels (cubic meters), of the following:

(1) The pipeline's maximum release time in hours, plus the maximum shutdown response time in hours (based on historic discharge data or in the absence of such historic data, the operator's best estimate), multiplied by the maximum flow rate expressed in barrels per hour (based on the maximum daily capacity of the pipeline), plus the largest line drainage volume after shutdown of the line section(s) in the response zone expressed in barrels (cubic meters); or

(2) The largest foreseeable discharge for the line section(s) within a response zone, expressed in barrels (cubic meters), based on the maximum historic discharge, if one exists, adjusted for any subsequent corrective or preventive action taken; or

(3) If the response zone contains one or more breakout tanks, the capacity of the single largest tank or battery of tanks within a single secondary containment system, adjusted for the capacity or size of the secondary containment system, expressed in barrels (cubic meters).

[58 FR 253, Jan. 5, 1993, as amended by Amdt. 194-3, 63 FR 37505, July 13, 1998]

**CAA RMP**

*Sec. 68.20 Applicability.*

Source: 61 FR 31718, June 20, 1996, unless otherwise noted.

The owner or operator of a stationary source subject to this part *shall* prepare a worst-case release scenario analysis as provided in Sec. 68.25 of this part and complete the five-year accident history as provided in Sec. 68.42. The owner or operator of a Program 2 and 3 process **must** comply with all sections in this subpart for these processes.

*Sec. 68.22 Offsite consequence analysis parameters.*

(a) Endpoints. For analyses of offsite consequences, the following endpoints *shall* be used:

(1) Toxics. The toxic endpoints provided in appendix A of this part.

(2) Flammables. The endpoints for flammables vary according to the scenarios studied:

(i) Explosion. An overpressure of 1 psi.

(ii) Radiant heat/exposure time. A radiant heat of 5 kw/m2 for 40 seconds.

(iii) Lower flammability limit. A lower flammability limit as provided in NFPA documents or other generally recognized sources.

(b) Wind speed/atmospheric stability class. For the worst-case release analysis, the owner or operator *shall* use a wind speed of 1.5 meters per second and F atmospheric stability class. If the owner or operator can demonstrate that local meteorological data applicable to the stationary source show a higher minimum wind speed or less stable atmosphere at all times during the previous three years, these minimums may be used. For analysis of alternative scenarios, the owner or operator may use the typical meteorological conditions for the stationary source.

(c) Ambient temperature/humidity. For worst-case release analysis of a regulated toxic substance, the owner or operator *shall* use the highest daily maximum temperature in the previous three years and average humidity for the site, based on temperature/humidity data gathered at the stationary source or at a local meteorological station; an owner or operator using the RMP Offsite Consequence Analysis Guidance may use 25 deg. C and 50 percent humidity as values for these variables. For analysis of alternative scenarios, the owner or operator may use typical temperature/humidity data gathered at the stationary source or at a local meteorological station.

(d) Height of release. The worst-case release of a regulated toxic substance *shall* be analyzed assuming a ground level (0 feet) release.

For an alternative scenario analysis of a regulated toxic substance, release height may be determined by the release scenario.

(e) Surface roughness. The owner or operator *shall* use either urban or rural topography, as appropriate. Urban means that there are many obstacles in the immediate area; obstacles include buildings or trees.

Rural means there are no buildings in the immediate area and the terrain is generally flat and unobstructed.

(f) Dense or neutrally buoyant gases. The owner or operator *shall* ensure that tables or models used for dispersion analysis of regulated toxic substances appropriately account for gas density.

(g) Temperature of released substance. For worst case, liquids other than gases liquefied by refrigeration only *shall* be considered to be released at the highest daily maximum temperature, based on data for the previous three years appropriate for the stationary source, or at process temperature, whichever is higher. For alternative scenarios, substances may be considered to be released at a process or ambient temperature that is appropriate for the scenario.

*Sec. 68.25 Worst-case release scenario analysis.*

(a) The owner or operator *shall* analyze and report in the RMP:

(1) For Program 1 processes, one worst-case release scenario for each Program 1 process;

(2) For Program 2 and 3 processes:

(i) One worst-case release scenario that is estimated to create the greatest distance in any direction to an endpoint provided in appendix A of this part resulting from an accidental release of regulated toxic substances from covered processes under worst-case conditions defined in Sec. 68.22;

(ii) One worst-case release scenario that is estimated to create the greatest distance in any direction to an endpoint defined in Sec. 68.22(a) resulting from an accidental release of regulated flammable substances from covered processes under worst-case conditions defined in Sec. 68.22; and

(iii) Additional worst-case release scenarios for a hazard class if a worst-case release from another covered process at the stationary source potentially affects public receptors different from those potentially affected by the worst-case release scenario developed under paragraphs (a)(2)(i) or (a)(2)(ii) of this section.

(b) Determination of worst-case release quantity. The worst-case release quantity *shall* be the greater of the following:

(1) For substances in a vessel, the greatest amount held in a single vessel, taking into account administrative controls that limit the maximum quantity; or

(2) For substances in pipes, the greatest amount in a pipe, taking into account administrative controls that limit the maximum quantity.

(c) Worst-case release scenario—toxic gases. (1) For regulated toxic substances that are normally gases at ambient temperature and handled as a gas or as a liquid under pressure, the owner or operator *shall* assume that the quantity in the vessel or pipe, as determined under paragraph (b) of this section, is released as a gas over 10 minutes. The release rate *shall* be assumed to be the total quantity divided by 10 unless passive mitigation systems are in place.

(2) For gases handled as refrigerated liquids at ambient pressure:

(i) If the released substance is not contained by passive mitigation systems or if the contained pool would have a depth of 1 cm or less, the owner or operator *shall* assume that the substance is released as a gas in 10 minutes;

(ii) If the released substance is contained by passive mitigation systems in a pool with a depth greater than 1 cm, the owner or operator may assume that the quantity in the vessel or pipe, as determined under paragraph (b) of this section, is spilled instantaneously to form a liquid pool. The volatilization rate (release rate) *shall* be calculated at the boiling point of the substance and at the conditions specified in paragraph (d) of this section.

(d) Worst-case release scenario—toxic liquids. (1) For regulated toxic substances that are normally liquids at ambient temperature, the owner or operator *shall* assume that the quantity in the vessel or pipe, as determined under paragraph (b) of this section, is spilled instantaneously to form a liquid pool.

(i) The surface area of the pool *shall* be determined by assuming that the liquid spreads to 1 centimeter deep unless passive mitigation systems are in place that serve to contain the spill and limit the surface area. Where passive mitigation is in place, the surface area of the contained liquid *shall* be used to calculate the volatilization rate.

(ii) If the release would occur onto a surface that is not paved or smooth, the owner or operator may take into account the actual surface characteristics.

(2) The volatilization rate *shall* account for the highest daily maximum temperature occurring in the past three years, the temperature of the substance in the vessel, and the concentration of the substance if the liquid spilled is a mixture or solution.

(3) The rate of release to air *shall* be determined from the volatilization rate of the liquid pool. The owner or operator may use the methodology in the RMP Offsite Consequence Analysis Guidance or any other publicly available techniques that account for the modeling conditions and are recognized by industry as applicable as part of current practices. Proprietary models that account for the modeling conditions may be used provided the owner or operator allows the implementing agency access to the model and describes model features and differences from publicly available models to local emergency planners upon request.

(e) Worst-case release scenario—flammable gases. The owner or operator *shall* assume that the quantity of the substance, as determined under paragraph (b) of this section and the provisions below, vaporizes resulting in a vapor cloud explosion. A yield factor of 10 percent of the available energy released in the explosion *shall* be used to determine the distance to the explosion endpoint if the model used is based on TNT equivalent methods.

(1) For regulated flammable substances that are normally gases at ambient temperature and handled as a gas or as a liquid under pressure, the owner or operator *shall* assume that the quantity in the vessel or pipe, as determined under paragraph (b) of this section, is released as a gas over 10 minutes. The total quantity *shall* be assumed to be involved in the vapor cloud explosion.

(2) For flammable gases handled as refrigerated liquids at ambient pressure:

(i) If the released substance is not contained by passive mitigation systems or if the contained pool would have a depth of one centimeter or less, the owner or operator *shall* assume that the total quantity of the substance is released as a gas in 10 minutes, and the total quantity will be involved in the vapor cloud explosion.

(ii) If the released substance is contained by passive mitigation systems in a pool with a depth greater than 1 centimeter, the owner or operator may assume that the quantity in the vessel or pipe, as determined under paragraph (b) of this section, is spilled instantaneously to form a liquid pool. The volatilization rate (release rate) *shall* be calculated at the boiling point of the substance and at the conditions specified in paragraph (d) of this section. The owner or operator *shall* assume that the quantity which becomes vapor in the first 10 minutes is involved in the vapor cloud explosion.

(f) Worst-case release scenario—flammable liquids. The owner or operator *shall* assume that the quantity of the substance, as determined under paragraph (b) of this section and the provisions below, vaporizes resulting in a vapor cloud explosion. A yield factor of 10 percent of the available energy released in the explosion *shall* be used to determine the distance to the explosion endpoint if the model used is based on TNT equivalent methods.

(1) For regulated flammable substances that are normally liquids at ambient temperature, the owner or operator *shall* assume that the entire quantity in the vessel or pipe, as determined under paragraph (b) of this section, is spilled instantaneously to form a liquid pool. For liquids at temperatures below their atmospheric boiling point, the volatilization rate *shall* be calculated at the conditions specified in paragraph (d) of this section.

(2) The owner or operator *shall* assume that the quantity which becomes vapor in the first 10 minutes is involved in the vapor cloud explosion.

(g) Parameters to be applied. The owner or operator *shall* use the parameters defined in Sec. 68.22 to determine distance to the endpoints.

The owner or operator may use the methodology provided in the RMP Offsite Consequence Analysis Guidance or any commercially or publicly available air dispersion modeling techniques, provided the techniques account for the modeling conditions and are recognized by industry as applicable as part of current practices. Proprietary models that account for the modeling conditions may be used provided the owner or operator allows the implementing agency access to the model and describes model features and differences from publicly available models to local emergency planners upon request.

(h) Consideration of passive mitigation. Passive mitigation systems may be considered for the analysis of worst case provided that the mitigation system is capable of withstanding the release event triggering the scenario and would still function as intended.

(i) Factors in selecting a worst-case scenario. Notwithstanding the provisions of paragraph (b) of this section, the owner or operator *shall* select as the worst case for flammable regulated substances or the worst case for regulated toxic substances, a scenario based on the following factors if such a scenario would result in a greater distance to an endpoint defined in Sec. 68.22(a) beyond the stationary source boundary than the scenario provided under paragraph (b) of this section:

(1) Smaller quantities handled at higher process temperature or pressure; and

(2) Proximity to the boundary of the stationary source.

[61 FR 31718, June 20, 1996, as amended at 64 FR 28700, May 26, 1999]

*Sec. 68.28 Alternative release scenario analysis.*

(a) The number of scenarios. The owner or operator *shall* identify and analyze at least one alternative release scenario for each regulated toxic substance held in a covered process(es) and at least one alternative release scenario to represent all flammable substances held in covered processes.

(b) Scenarios to consider. (1) For each scenario required under paragraph (a) of this section, the owner or operator *shall* select a scenario:

(i) That is more likely to occur than the worst-case release scenario under Sec. 68.25; and

(ii) That will reach an endpoint offsite, unless no such scenario exists.

(2) Release scenarios considered should include, but are not limited to, the following, where applicable:

(i) Transfer hose releases due to splits or sudden hose uncoupling;

(ii) Process piping releases from failures at flanges, joints, welds, valves and valve seals, and drains or bleeds;

(iii) Process vessel or pump releases due to cracks, seal failure, or drain, bleed, or plug failure;

(iv) Vessel overfilling and spill, or over pressurization and venting through relief valves or rupture disks; and

(v) Shipping container mishandling and breakage or puncturing leading to a spill.

(c) Parameters to be applied. The owner or operator *shall* use the appropriate parameters defined in Sec. 68.22 to determine distance to the endpoints. The owner or operator may use either the methodology provided in the RMP Offsite Consequence Analysis Guidance or any commercially or publicly available air dispersion modeling techniques, provided the techniques account for the specified modeling conditions and are recognized by industry as applicable as part of current practices. Proprietary models that account for the modeling conditions may be used provided the owner or operator allows the implementing agency access to the model and describes model features and differences from publicly available models to local emergency planners upon request.

(d) Consideration of mitigation. Active and passive mitigation systems may be considered provided they are capable of withstanding the event that triggered the release and would still be functional.

(e) Factors in selecting scenarios. The owner or operator *shall* consider the following in selecting alternative release scenarios:

(1) The five-year accident history provided in Sec. 68.42; and

(2) Failure scenarios identified under Sec. 68.50 or Sec. 68.67.

*Sec. 68.30 Defining offsite impacts—populationn.*

(a) The owner or operator *shall* estimate in the RMP the population within a circle with its center at the point of the release and a radius determined by the distance to the endpoint defined in Sec. 68.22(a).

(b) Population to be defined. Population *shall* include residential population. The presence of institutions (schools, hospitals, prisons), parks and recreational areas, and major commercial, office, and industrial buildings *shall* be noted in the RMP.

(c) Data sources acceptable. The owner or operator may use the most recent Census data, or other updated information, to estimate the population potentially affected.

(d) Level of accuracy. Population *shall* be estimated to two significant digits.

*Sec. 68.33 Defining offsite impacts—environmentt.*

(a) The owner or operator *shall* list in the RMP environmental receptors within a circle with its center at the point of the release and a radius determined by the distance to the endpoint defined in Sec. 68.22(a) of this part.

(b) Data sources acceptable. The owner or operator may rely on information provided on local U.S. Geological Survey maps or on any data source containing U.S.G.S. data to identify environmental receptors.

*Sec. 68.36 Review and update.*

(a) The owner or operator *shall* review and update the offsite consequence analyses at least once every five years.

(b) If changes in processes, quantities stored or handled, or any other aspect of the stationary source might reasonably be expected to increase or decrease the distance to the endpoint by a factor of two or more, the owner or operator *shall* complete a revised analysis within six months of the change and submit a revised risk management plan as provided in Sec. 68.190.

*Sec. 68.50 Hazard review.*

(a) The owner or operator *shall* conduct a review of the hazards associated with the regulated substances, process, and procedures. The review *shall* identify the following:

(1) The hazards associated with the process and regulated substances;

(2) Opportunities for equipment malfunctions or human errors that could cause an accidental release;

(3) The safeguards used or needed to control the hazards or prevent equipment malfunction or human error; and

(4) Any steps used or needed to detect or monitor releases.

(b) The owner or operator may use checklists developed by persons or organizations knowledgeable about the process and equipment as a guide to conducting the review. For processes designed to meet industry standards or Federal or state design rules, the hazard review *shall*, by inspecting all equipment, determine whether the process is designed, fabricated, and operated in accordance with the applicable standards or rules.

(c) The owner or operator *shall* document the results of the review and ensure that problems identified are resolved in a timely manner.

(d) The review *shall* be updated at least once every five years. The owner or operator *shall* also conduct reviews whenever a major change in the process occurs; all issues identified in the review *shall* be resolved before startup of the changed process.

*Sec. 68.67 Process hazard analysis.*

(a) The owner or operator *shall* perform an initial process hazard analysis (hazard evaluation) on processes covered by this part. The process hazard analysis *shall* be appropriate to the complexity of the process and *shall* identify, evaluate, and control the hazards involved in the process. The owner or operator *shall* determine and document the priority order for conducting process hazard analyses based on a rationale which includes such considerations as extent of the process hazards, number of potentially affected employees, age of the process, and operating history of the process. The process hazard analysis *shall* be conducted as soon as possible, but not later than June 21, 1999.

Process hazards analyses completed to comply with 29 CFR 1910.119(e) are acceptable as initial process hazards analyses. These process hazard analyses *shall* be updated and revalidated, based on their completion date.

(b) The owner or operator *shall* use one or more of the following methodologies that are appropriate to determine and evaluate the hazards of the process being analyzed.

(1) What-If;

(2) Checklist;

(3) What-If/Checklist;

(4) Hazard and Operability Study (HAZOP);

(5) Failure Mode and Effects Analysis (FMEA);

(6) Fault Tree Analysis; or

(7) An appropriate equivalent methodology.

(c) The process hazard analysis *shall* address:

(1) The hazards of the process;

(2) The identification of any previous incident which had a likely potential for catastrophic consequences.

(3) Engineering and administrative controls applicable to the hazards and their interrelationships such as appropriate application of detection methodologies to provide early warning of releases. (Acceptable detection methods might include process monitoring and control instrumentation with alarms, and detection hardware such as hydrocarbon sensors.);

(4) Consequences of failure of engineering and administrative controls;

(5) Stationary source siting;

(6) Human factors; and

(7) A qualitative evaluation of a range of the possible safety and health effects of failure of controls.

(d) The process hazard analysis *shall* be performed by a team with expertise in engineering and process operations, and the team *shall* include at least one employee who has experience and knowledge specific to the process being evaluated. Also, one member of the team **must** be knowledgeable in the specific process hazard analysis methodology being used.

(e) The owner or operator *shall* establish a system to promptly address the team's findings and recommendations; assure that the recommendations are resolved in a timely manner and that the resolution is documented; document what actions are to be taken; complete actions as soon as possible; develop a written schedule of when these actions are to be completed; communicate the actions to operating, maintenance and other employees whose work assignments are in the process and who may be affected by the recommendations or actions.

(f) At least every five (5) years after the completion of the initial process hazard analysis, the process hazard analysis *shall* be updated and revalidated by a team meeting the requirements in paragraph (d) of this section, to assure that the process hazard analysis is consistent with the current process. Updated and revalidated process hazard analyses completed to comply with 29 CFR 1910.119(e) are acceptable to meet the requirements of this paragraph.

(g) The owner or operator *shall* retain process hazards analyses and updates or revalidations for each process covered by this section, as well as the documented resolution of recommendations described in paragraph (e) of this section for the life of the process.

### A.3.4.2 Protection

This section of Annex 3 should present a discussion of strategies for protecting the vulnerable receptors identified through the hazard analysis. Primary consideration should be given to minimizing those risks identified as a high priority. Activities to be considered in developing this section include: population protection; protective booming; dispersant use, in-situ burning, bioremediation; water intake protection; wildlife recovery/rehabilitation; natural remediation; vapor suppression; and monitoring, sampling, and modeling. ACPs and LEPC plans may contain much of this information.

| RCRA (40 CFR part 264, Subpart D, 40 CFR Part 265, Subpart D, and 40 CFR 279.52 | EPA's Oil Pollution Prevention Regulation (40 CFR Part 112) | USCG-FRG (33 CFR Part 154) | OSHA HAZWOPER (29 CFR 1910.120) |
|---|---|---|---|
| | 112.20(h)(7)(i) 112.20(h)(7)(iv) F1.7.1, F1.7.3 | 1035(b)(4) | (l)(1)(iv)(v),(vi) (p)(8)(ii)(D),(E),(K) (q)(2)(iv),(v),(vi) (q)(3)(iii) |

## EPA's Oil Pollution Prevention Regulation

*Response Resources for Small, Medium, and Worst Case Discharges (Appendix F1.7.1)*

Once the discharge scenarios have been identified in section 1.5 of the response plan, the facility owner or operator *shall* identify and describe implementation of the response actions. The facility owner or operator *shall* demonstrate accessibility to the proper response personnel and equipment to effectively respond to all of the identified discharge scenarios. The determination and demonstration of adequate response capability are presented in Appendix E to this part. In addition, steps to expedite the clean-up of oil discharges **must** be discussed. At a minimum, the following items **must** be ad-dressed:

(1) Emergency plans for spill response;
(2) Additional response training;
(3) Additional contracted help;
(4) Access to additional response equipment/experts; and
(5) Ability to implement the plan including response training and practice drills.

1.7.1.2A recommended form detailing immediate actions follows.

OIL SPILL RESPONSE—IMMEDIATE ACTIONS
1. Stop the product flow. Act quickly to secure pumps, close valves, etc.
2. Warn personnel. Enforce safety and security measures.
3. Shut off ignition sources. Motors, electrical circuits, open flames, etc.
4. Initiate containment. Around the tank and/or in the water with oil boom.
5. Notify NRC. 1–800–424–8802
6. Notify OSC
7. Notify, as appropriate
Source: FOSS, Oil Spill Response—Emergency Procedures, Revised December 3, 1992.

## A.3.4.3 Coordination With Material Resource Trustees

This section should address coordination with government natural resource trustees. In their role as managers of and experts in natural resources, trustees assist the federal OSC in developing or selecting removal actions to protect these resources. In this role, they serve as part of the response organization working for the federal OSC. A key area to address is interaction with facility response personnel in protection of natural resources.

Natural resource trustees are also responsible to act on behalf of the public to present a claim for and recover damages to natural resources injured by an oil spill or hazardous substance release. The process followed by the natural resource trustees, natural resource damage assessment (NRDA), generally involves some data collection during emergency response. NRDA regulations provide that the process may be carried out in cooperation with the responsible party. Thus, the facility may wish to plan for how that cooperation will occur, including designation of personnel to work with trustees in NRDA.

| RCRA (40 CFR part 264, Subpart D, 40 CFR Part 265, Subpart D, and 40 CFR 279.52 | EPA's Oil Pollution Prevention Regulation (40 CFR Part 112) | USCG-FRG (33 CFR Part 154) | DOT/RSPA-FRP (49 CFR part 194) | OSHA Emergency Action Plans (29 CFR 1910.38(a)) and Process Safety (29 CFR 1910.119) |
|---|---|---|---|---|
| | 112.20(g) | 1035(f) | 194.107(c) | |

## EPA's Oil Pollution Prevention Regulation

*EPA (40 CFR 112.20(g))*

All facility response plans *shall* be consistent with the requirements of the National Oil and Hazardous Substance Pollution Contingency Plan (40 CFR part 300) and applicable Area Contingency Plans prepared pursuant to section 311(j)(4) of the Clean Water Act. The facility response plan should be coordinated with the local emergency response plan developed by the local emergency planning committee under section 303 of Title III of the Superfund Amendments and Reauthorization Act of 1986 (42 U.S.C. 11001 et seq.). Upon request, the owner or operator should provide a copy of the facility response plan to the local emergency planning committee or State emergency response commission.

The owner or operator *shall* review relevant portions of the National Oil and Hazardous Substances Pollution Contingency Plan and applicable Area Contingency Plan annually and, if necessary, revise the facility response plan to ensure consistency with these plans.

The owner or operator *shall* review and update the facility response plan periodically to reflect changes at the facility.

## DOT/RSPA-FRP

*(49 CFR 194.107(c))*

Each response plan **must** be consistent with the National Contingency Plan (NCP) (40 CFR part 300) and each applicable Area Contingency Plan (ACP). An operator **must** certify that it has reviewed the NCP and each applicable ACP and that its response plan is consistent with the existing NCP and each existing applicable ACP.

## USCG-FRG

*(33 CFR Part 154.1035(f))*

The information contained in a response plan **must** be consistent with the National Oil and Hazardous Substances Pollution Contingency Plan (NCP) (40 CFR part 300) and the Area Contingency Plan(s) (ACP) covering the area in which the facility operates. Facility owners or operators *shall* ensure that their response plans are in accordance with the ACP in effect 6 months prior to initial plan submission or the annual plan review required under Sec. 154.1065(a). Facility owners or operators are not required to, but may at their option, conform to an ACP which is less than 6 months old at the time of plan submission.

### A.3.4.4 Waste Management

This section should address procedures for the disposal of contaminated materials in accordance with federal, state, and local requirements.

| RCRA (40 CFR part 264, Subpart D, 40 CFR Part 265, Subpart D, and 40 CFR 279.52 | EPA's Oil Pollution Prevention Regulation (40 CFR Part 112) | USCG-FRG (33 CFR Part 154) | DOT/RSPA-FRP (49 CFR part 194) |
|---|---|---|---|
| 264.56(h)(1) 265.56(h)(1) 279.52(b)(6)(viii)(A) 264.56(g) 265.56(g) 279.52(b)(6)(vii) | 112.20(h)(7)(iv) F1.7.2 | 1035(b)(5) | 194.107(d)(1)(v) |

## RCRA

*(40 CFR 264.56(g) and (h)(1))*

Immediately after an emergency, the emergency coordinator **must** provide for treating, storing, or disposing of recovered waste, contaminated soil or surface water, or any other material that results from a release, fire, or explosion at the facility.

[Comment: Unless the owner or operator can demonstrate, in accordance with Sec. 261.3(c) or (d) of this chapter, that the recovered material is not a hazardous waste, the owner or operator becomes a generator of hazardous waste and **must** manage it in accordance with all applicable requirements of parts 262, 263, and 264 of this chapter.]

The emergency coordinator **must** ensure that, in the affected area(s) of the facility:

(1) No waste that may be incompatible with the released material is treated, stored, or disposed of until cleanup procedures are completed.

## A.3.5 Logistics

(1) Medical needs of responders
(2) Site security

(3) Communications (internal and external resources)
(4) Transportation (air, land, water)
(5) Personnel support (e.g., meals, housing, equipment)
(6) Equipment maintenance and support

This section of the Annex 3 should address how the facility will provide for the operational needs of response operations in each of the areas listed above. For example, the discussion of personnel support should address issues such as: volunteer training; management; overnight accommodations; meals; operational/administrative spaces; and emergency procedures. The NRT recognizes that certain logistical considerations may not be applicable to small facilities with limited hazards.

| USCG-FRG (33 CFR Part 154) | DOT/RSPA-FRP (49 CFR part 194) | OSHA Emergency Action Plans (29 CFR 1910.38(a)) and Process Safety (29 CFR 1910.119) | OSHA HAZWOPER (29 CFR 1910.120) | CAA RMP (40 CFR part 68) |
| --- | --- | --- | --- | --- |
| 1035(b)(3)(iii) | | | (l)(3)(iii) (p)(8)(iv)(B) (q)(2)(xii) | |

## OSHA HAZWOPER

*OSHA (29 CFR 1910.120(q)(2)(xii))*

Emergency response organizations may use the local emergency response plan or the state emergency response plan or both, as part of their emergency response plan to avoid duplication. Those items of the emergency response plan that are being properly addressed by the SARA Title III plans may be substituted into their emergency plan or otherwise kept together for the employer and employee's use.

## A.3.5.1 Medical Needs

| USCG-FRG (33 CFR Part 154) | OSHA Emergency Action Plans (29 CFR 1910.38(a)) and Process Safety (29 CFR 1910.119) | OSHA HAZWOPER (29 CFR 1910.120) | CAA RMP (40 CFR part 68) |
|---|---|---|---|
| 1035(e)(5) | 38(a)(2)(iv) | (l)(2)(viii) (p)(8)(ii)(H) (q)(2)(vii) | 68.95(a)(1)(ii) |

### USCG-FRG

*(33 CFR 154.1035(e)(5))*
*Site-specific safety and health plan.*

This appendix **must** describe the safety and health plan to be implemented for any response location(s). It **must** provide as much detailed information as is practicable in advance of an actual discharge. This appendix may reference another existing plan requiring under 29 CFR 1910.120.

### OSHA Emergency Action Plans

*(29 CFR 1910.38(a)(2)(iv))*

Rescue and medical duties for those employees who are to perform them.

### CAA-RMP

*(40 CFR 68.95(a)(1)(ii))*

Documentation of proper first-aid and emergency medical treatment necessary to treat accidental human exposures.

## A.3.5.2 Site Security

| RCRA (40 CFR part 264, Subpart D, 40 CFR Part 265, Subpart D, and 40 CFR 279.52 | EPA's Oil Pollution Prevention Regulation (40 CFR Part 112) | OSHA HAZWOPER (29 CFR 1910.120) | CAA RMP (40 CFR part 68) |
|---|---|---|---|
| | 112.20(h)(10) F1.10 | (l)(2)(v) (p)(8)(ii)(E) (q)(2)(v) | |

### EPA's Oil Pollution Prevention

*EPA (40 CFR 112.20(h)(10) and Appendix F 1.10)*

*Emergency Response Action Plan*

Several sections of the response plan *shall* be co-located for easy access by response personnel during an actual emergency or oil discharge. This collection of sections *shall* be called the Emergency Response Action Plan. The Agency intends that the Action Plan contain only as much information as is necessary to combat the discharge and be arranged so response actions are not delayed. The Action Plan may be arranged in a number of ways. For example, the sections of the Emergency Response Action Plan may be photocopies or condensed versions of the forms included in the associated sections of the response plan. Each Emergency Response Action Plan section may be tabbed for quick reference. The Action Plan *shall* be maintained in the front of the same binder that contains the complete response plan or it *shall* be contained in a separate binder. In the latter case, both binders *shall* be kept together so that the entire plan can be accessed by the qualified individual and appropriate spill response personnel. The Emergency Response Action Plan *shall* be made up of the following sections:

1. Qualified Individual Information (Section 1.2) partial
2. Emergency Notification Phone List (Section 1.3.1) partial
3. Spill Response Notification Form (Section 1.3.1) partial
4. Response Equipment List and Location (Section 1.3.2) complete
5. Response Equipment Testing and Deployment (Section 1.3.3) complete
6. Facility Response Team (Section 1.3.4) partial
7. Evacuation Plan (Section 1.3.5) condensed
8. Immediate Actions (Section 1.7.1) complete
9. Facility Diagram (Section 1.9) complete

## A.3.5.3 Communications

| EPA's Oil Pollution Prevention Regulation (40 CFR Part 112) | USCG-FRG (33 CFR Part 154) | DOT/RSPA-FRP (49 CFR part 194) | OSHA Emergency Action Plans (29 CFR 1910.38(a)) and Process Safety (29 CFR 1910.119) | OSHA HAZWOPER (29 CFR 1910.120) |
|---|---|---|---|---|
| 112.20(h)(1)(iv) 112.20(h)(3)(vi) F1.3.2 | 1035(e)(3) | 194.107(d)(1)(v) A-2 | 38(a)(3) 119(e)(3)(iii) 165(b) | (q)(3)(i) |

**EEPA's Oil Pollution Prevention**

*EPA (40 CFR 112.20(h)(1)(iv); (h)(3)(vi) and Appendix F1.3.2)*

8) ☐ Communication Equipment (include operating frequency and channel and/or cellular phone numbers)—Operation Status:

| Type and Year | Quantity | Storage Location/Number |
|---|---|---|
| | | |
| | | |
| | | |

## OSHA Fire Protection

*General requirements (29 CFR 1910.165(b)).*

The employee alarm system *shall* provide warning for necessary emergency action as called for in the emergency action plan, or for reaction time for safe escape of employees from the workplace or the immediate work area, or both.

The employee alarm *shall* be capable of being perceived above ambient noise or light levels by all employees in the affected portions of the workplace. Tactile devices may be used to alert those employees who would not otherwise be able to recognize the audible or visual alarm.

The employee alarm *shall* be distinctive and recognizable as a signal to evacuate the work area or to perform actions designated under the emergency action plan.

The employer *shall* explain to each employee the preferred means of reporting emergencies, such as manual pull box alarms, public address systems, radio or telephones. The employer *shall* post emergency telephone numbers near telephones, or employee notice boards, and other conspicuous locations when telephones serve as a means of reporting emergencies. Where a communication system also serves as the employee alarm system, all emergency messages *shall* have priority over all non-emergency messages.

The employer *shall* establish procedures for sounding emergency alarms in the workplace. For those employers with 10 or fewer employees in a particular workplace, direct voice communication is an acceptable procedure for sounding the alarm provided all employees can hear the alarm. Such workplaces need not have a back-up system.

## A.3.5.4 Transportation

| RCRA (40 CFR part 264, Subpart D, 40 CFR Part 265, Subpart D, and 40 CFR 279.52 | EPA's Oil Pollution Prevention Regulation (40 CFR Part 112) | USCG-FRG (33 CFR Part 154) | DOT/RSPA-FRP (49 CFR part 194) | OSHA Emergency Action Plans (29 CFR 1910.38(a)) and Process Safety (29 CFR 1910.119) | OSHA HAZWOPER (29 CFR 1910.120) | CAA RMP (40 CFR part 68) |
|---|---|---|---|---|---|---|
| | | | | | | |

Generally, government and/or personal vehicles or commercial airlines are utilized as transportation during response incidents. If necessary, charter services may be contracted.

*For further information, see the* **NOAA HAZMAT First Class User's Manual,** *dated June 1994, or contact (202) 267-4497.*

*For information concerning procedures for logging onto the system and for reading reports, contact ORSANCO at (513) 231-7719.*

## A.3.5.5 Personnel Support

| RCRA (40 CFR part 264, Subpart D, 40 CFR Part 265, Subpart D, and 40 CFR 279.52 | EPA's Oil Pollution Prevention Regulation (40 CFR Part 112) | OSHA Emergency Action Plans (29 CFR 1910.38(a)) and Process Safety (29 CFR 1910.119) | OSHA HAZWOPER (29 CFR 1910.120) |
|---|---|---|---|
| | 112.20(h)(1)(v) 112.20(h)(1)(vi) 112.20(h)(3)(i-ii) 112.20(h)(3)(v) 112.20(h)(3)(vii) F1.3.5 | 38(a)(5)(i) | (l)(2)(ii) (p)(8)(ii)(B) (q)(2)(ii) (q)(3)(v)(vi) |

## EPA's Oil Pollution Prevention Regulation

*Emergency response action plan and Information about emergency response*

A description of response personnel capabilities, including the duties of persons at the facility during a response action and their response times and qualifications;

Plans for evacuation of the facility and a reference to community evacuation plans, as appropriate

The identity of private personnel and equipment necessary to remove to the maximum extent practicable a worst case discharge and other discharges of oil described in paragraph (h)(5) of this section, and to mitigate or prevent a substantial threat of a worst case discharge (To identify response resources to meet the facility response plan requirements of this section, owners or operators *shall* follow Appendix E to this part or, where not appropriate, *shall* clearly demonstrate in the response plan why use of Appendix E of this part is not appropriate at the facility and make comparable arrangements for response resources);

Evidence of contracts or other approved means for ensuring the availability of such personnel and equipment;

A description of response personnel capabilities, including the duties of persons at the facility during a response action and their response times and qualifications

Plans for evacuation of the facility and a reference to community evacuation plans, as appropriate

*Evacuation Plans*

Based on the analysis of the facility, as discussed elsewhere in the plan, a facility-wide evacuation plan *shall* be developed. In addition, plans to evacuate parts of the facility that are at a high risk of exposure in the event of a discharge or other release **must** be developed. Evacuation routes **must** be shown on a diagram of the facility (see section 1.9 of this appendix). When developing evacuation plans, consideration **must** be given to the following factors, as appropriate:

(1) Location of stored materials;

(2) Hazard imposed by discharged material;

(3) Discharge flow direction;

(4) Prevailing wind direction and speed;

(5) Water currents, tides, or wave conditions (if applicable);

(6) Arrival route of emergency response personnel and response equipment;

(7) Evacuation routes;

(8) Alternative routes of evacuation;

(9) Transportation of injured personnel to nearest emergency medical facility;

(10) Location of alarm/notification systems;

(11) The need for a centralized check-in area for evacuation validation (roll call);

(12) Selection of a mitigation command center; and

(13) Location of shelter at the facility as an alternative to evacuation.

One resource that may be helpful to owners or operators in preparing this section of the response plan is The Handbook of Chemical Hazard Analysis Procedures by the Federal Emergency Management Agency (FEMA), Department of Transportation (DOT), and EPA. The Handbook of Chemical Hazard Analysis Procedures is available from: FEMA , Publication Office, 500 C. Street, S.W., Washington, DC 20472, (202) 646-3484.

As specified in Sec. 112.20(h)(1)(vi), the facility owner or operator **must** reference existing community evacuation plans, as appropriate.

## OSHA Emergency Action Plans

*Training*

Before implementing the emergency action plan, the employer *shall* designate and train a sufficient number of persons to assist in the safe and orderly emergency evacuation of employees.

## OSHA HAZWOPER

The individual in charge of the ICS *shall* limit the number of emergency response personnel at the emergency site, in those areas of potential or actual exposure to incident or site hazards, to those who are actively performing emergency operations. However, operations in hazardous areas *shall* be performed using the buddy system in groups of two or more.

Back-up personnel *shall* stand by with equipment ready to provide assistance or rescue. Advance first aid support personnel, as a minimum, *shall* also stand by with medical equipment and transportation capability.

## A.3.5.6 Equipment Maintenance and Support

| EPA's Oil Pollution Prevention Regulation (40 CFR Part 112) | USCG-FRG (33 CFR Part 154) | DOT/RSPA-FRP (49 CFR part 194) | OSHA Emergency Action Plans (29 CFR 1910.38(a)) and Process Safety (29 CFR 1910.119) | OSHA HAZWOPER (29 CFR 1910.120) | CAA RMP (40 CFR part 68) |
|---|---|---|---|---|---|
| 112.20(h)(1)(iv) 112.20(h)(3)(vi) 112.20(h)(8) F1.3.3 F1.8.1 | 1035(b)(3)(iv) 1035(e)(3) 1057 | 194.107(d)(1(vii) | 119(j)(4) 119(j)(5) 165(d) | (l)(2)(xi) (p)(8)(ii)(K) (q)(2)(xi) | 68.95(a)(2) |

## EPA'S Oil Pollution Prevention Regulation

*Response Equipment Testing/Deployment*

Date of Last Update:_____

Response Equipment Testing and Deployment Drill Log

Last Inspection or Response Equipment Test Date:_____
Inspection Frequency:_____
Last Deployment Drill Date:_____
Deployment Frequency:_____
Oil Spill Removal Organization Certification (if applicable):_____

*Facility Self-Inspection*

Pursuant to 40 CFR 112.7(e)(8), each facility *shall* include the written procedures and records of inspections in the SPCC Plan. The inspection *shall* include the tanks, secondary containment, and response equipment at the facility. Records of the inspections of tanks and secondary containment required by 40 CFR 112.7(e) *shall* be cross-referenced in the response plan. The inspection of response equipment is a new requirement in this plan. Facility self-inspection requires two steps: (1) a checklist of things to inspect; and (2) a method of recording the actual inspection and its findings. The date of each inspection *shall* be noted. These records are required to be maintained for 5 years.

## USCG-FRP

*Inspection and maintenance of response resources.*

A facility owner or operator required to submit a response plan under this part **must** ensure that—

Containment booms, skimmers, vessels, and other major equipment listed or referenced in the plan are periodically inspected and maintained in good operating condition, in accordance with manufacturer's recommendations, and best commercial practices; and

All inspection and maintenance is documented and that these records are maintained for 3 years.

For equipment which **must** be inspected and maintained under this section the Coast Guard may—

(1) Verify that the equipment inventories exist as represented;

(2) Verify the existences of records required under this section;

(3) Verify that the records of inspection and maintenance reflect the actual condition of any equipment listed or referenced; and

(4) Inspect and require operational tests of equipment.

This section does not apply to containment booms, skimmers, vessels, and other major equipment listed or referenced in the plan and ensured available from an oil spill removal organization through the written consent required under Sec. 154.1028(a)(5).

## OSHA Process Safety

*Inspection and testing (29 CFR 1910.119(j)(4)).*

Inspections and tests *shall* be performed on process equipment.

Inspection and testing procedures *shall* follow recognized and generally accepted good engineering practices.

The frequency of inspections and tests of process equipment *shall* be consistent with applicable manufacturers' recommendations and good engineering practices, and more frequently if determined to be necessary by prior operating experience.

The employer *shall* document each inspection and test that has been performed on process equipment. The documentation *shall* identify the date of the inspection or test, the name of the person who performed the inspection or test, the serial number or other identifier of the equipment on which the inspection or test was performed, a description of the inspection or test performed, and the results of the inspection or test.

*Equipment deficiencies (29 CFR 1910.119(j)(5)).*

The employer *shall* correct deficiencies in equipment that are outside acceptable limits (defined by the process safety information in paragraph

(d) of this section) before further use or in a safe and timely manner when necessary means are taken to assure safe operation.

**OSHA Fire Protection**

*Maintenance and testing (29 CFR 1910.165(d)).*

The employer *shall* assure that all employee alarm systems are maintained in operating condition except when undergoing repairs or maintenance.

The employer *shall* assure that a test of the reliability and adequacy of non-supervised employee alarm systems is made every two months. A different actuation device *shall* be used in each test of a multi-actuation device system so that no individual device is used for two consecutive tests.

The employer *shall* maintain or replace power supplies as often as is necessary to assure a fully operational condition. Back-up means of alarm, such as employee runners or telephones, *shall* be provided when systems are out of service.

The employer *shall* assure that employee alarm circuitry installed after January 1, 1981, which is capable of being supervised is supervised and that it will provide positive notification to assigned personnel whenever a deficiency exists in the system. The employer *shall* assure that all supervised employee alarm systems are tested at least annually for reliability and adequacy.

The employer *shall* assure that the servicing, maintenance and testing of employee alarms are done by persons trained in the designed operation and functions necessary for reliable and safe operation of the system.

## A.3.6 Finance/Procurement/Administration

(1) Resource list(2) Personnel management
(3) Response equipment
(4) Support equipment
(5) Contracting

(6) Claims procedures
(7) Cost documentation

This section of Annex 3 should address the acquisition of resources (i.e., personnel and equipment) for the response and monitoring of incident-related costs. Lists of available equipment in the local and regional area and how to procure such equipment as necessary should be included. Information on previously established agreements (e.g., contracts) with organizations supplying personnel and equipment (e.g., oil spill removal organizations) also should be included. This section should also address methods to account for resources expended and to process claims resulting from the incident.

| RCRA (40 CFR part 264, Subpart D, 40 CFR Part 265, Subpart D, and 40 CFR 279.52 | EPA's Oil Pollution Prevention Regulation (40 CFR Part 112) | USCG-FRG (33 CFR Part 154) |
|---|---|---|
| | 112.20(h)(3)(ix) | 1035(b)(3)(iii) 1028 |

**USCG-FRG**

*(33 CFR 154.1028)*

*Methods of ensuring the availability of response resources by contract or other approved means.*

When required in this subpart, the availability of response resources <u>must</u> be ensured by the following methods:
(1) A written contractual agreement with an oil spill removal organization. The agreement <u>must</u> identify and ensure the availability of specified personnel and equipment required under this subpart within stipulated response times in the specified geographic areas;

(2) Certification by the facility owner or operator that specified personnel and equipment required under this subpart are owned, operated, or under the direct control of the facility owner or operator, and are available within stipulated response times in the specified geographic areas;

(3) Active membership in a local or regional oil spill removal organization that has identified specified personnel and equipment required under this subpart that are available to respond to a discharge within stipulated response times in the specified geographic areas;

(4) A document which—

(i) Identifies the personnel, equipment, and services capable of being provided by the oil spill removal organization within stipulated response times in the specified geographic areas;

(ii) Sets out the parties' acknowledgment that the oil spill removal organization intends to commit the resources in the event of a response;

(iii) Permits the Coast Guard to verify the availability of the identified response resources through tests, inspections, and drills; and

(iv) Is referenced in the response plan; or

(5) The identification of an oil spill removal organization with specified equipment and personnel available within stipulated response times in specified geographic areas. The organization **must** provide written consent to being identified in the plan.

(b) The contracts and documents required in paragraph (a) of this section **must** be retained at the facility and **must** be produced for review upon request by the COTP.

## A.3.6.1 Resource List

| RCRA (40 CFR part 264, Subpart D, 40 CFR Part 265, Subpart D, and 40 CFR 279.52 | EPA's Oil Pollution Prevention Regulation (40 CFR Part 112) | USCG-FRG (33 CFR Part 154) | DOT/RSPA-FRP (49 CFR part 194) |
|---|---|---|---|
| 264.52(e) 265.52(e) 279.52(b)(2)(v) | 112.20(h)(1)(iv) 112.20(h)(3)(vi) F1.3.2 F1.7.1 | 1035(b)(3)(iv) 1035(e)(3) | |

## RCRA

The plan **must** include a list of all emergency equipment at the facility (such as fire extinguishing systems, spill control equipment, communications and alarm systems (internal and external), and decontamination equipment), where this equipment is required. This list **must** be kept up to date. In addition, the plan **must** include the location and a physical description of each item on the list, and a brief outline of its capabilities.

### EPA's Oil Prevention Regulation

Section 1.3.2 provides a description of the facility's list of emergency response equipment and location of the response equipment.

When appropriate, the amount of oil that emergency response equipment can handle and any limitations (e.g., launching sites) **must** be described.

*Response Resources for Small, Medium, and Worst Case Discharges*

Once the discharge scenarios have been identified in section 1.5 of the response plan, the facility owner or operator *shall* identify and describe implementation of the response actions. The facility owner or operator *shall* demonstrate accessibility to the proper response personnel and equipment to effectively respond to all of the identified discharge scenarios. The determination and demonstration of adequate response capability are presented in Appendix E to this part.

In addition, steps to expedite the cleanup of oil discharges **must** be discussed. At a minimum, the following items **must** be addressed:
(1) Emergency plans for spill response;
(2) Additional response training;
(3) Additional contracted help;
(4) Access to additional response equipment/experts; and
(5) Ability to implement the plan including response training and practice drills.

## USCG-FRP

This subsection **must** identify the oil spill removal organizations and the spill management team to:
Be capable of providing the following response resources:

(1) Equipment and supplies to meet the requirements of Secs. 154.1045, 154.1047 or subparts H or I of this part, as appropriate; and
(2) Trained personnel necessary to continue operation of the equipment and staff of the oil spill removal organization and spill management team for the first 7 days of the response.

This section **must** include job descriptions for each spill management team member within the organizational structure described in paragraph (b)(3)(iii) of this section. These job descriptions should include the responsibilities and duties of each spill management team member in a response action.

For mobile facilities that operate in more than one COTP zone, the plan **must** identify the oil spill removal organization and the spill management team in the applicable geographic-specific appendix. The oil spill removal organization(s) and the spill management team discussed in paragraph (b)(3)(iv)(A) of this section **must** be included for each COTP zone in which the facility will handle, store, or transport oil in bulk.

*Equipment list and records.*

This appendix **must** include the information specified in this paragraph.
The appendix **must** contain a list of equipment and facility personnel required to respond to an average most probable discharge, as defined in Sec. 154.1020. The appendix **must** also list the location of the equipment.

The appendix **must** contain a detailed listing of all the major equipment identified in the plan as belonging to an oil spill removal organization(s) that is available, by contract or other approved means as described in Sec. 154.1028(a), to respond to a maximum most probable or worst case discharge, as defined in Sec. 154.1020. The detailed listing of all major equipment may be located in a separate document referenced by the plan. Either the appendix or the separate document referenced in the plan **must** provide the location of the major response equipment.

It is not necessary to list response equipment from oil spill removal organization(s) when the organization has been classified by the Coast Guard and their capacity has been determined to equal or exceed the response capability needed by the facility. For oil spill removal organization(s) classified by the Coast Guard, the classification **must** be noted in this section of the plan. When it is necessary for the appendix to contain a listing of response equipment, it *shall* include all of the following items that are identified in the response plan:

Skimmers; booms; dispersant application, in-situ burning, bioremediation equipment and supplies, and other equipment used to apply other chemical agents on the NCP Product Schedule (if applicable); communications, firefighting, and beach cleaning equipment; boats and motors; disposal and storage equipment; and heavy equipment. The list **must** include for each piece of equipment—

(A) The type, make, model, and year of manufacture listed on the nameplate of the equipment;
(B) For oil recovery devices, the effective daily recovery rate, as determined using section 6 of Appendix C of this part;
(C) For containment boom, the overall boom height (draft and freeboard) and type of end connectors;

(D) The spill scenario in which the equipment will be used for or which it is contracted;

(E) The total daily capacity for storage and disposal of recovered oil;

(F) For communication equipment, the type and amount of equipment intended for use during response activities. Where applicable, the primary and secondary radio frequencies **must** be specified.

(G) Location of the equipment; and

(H) The date of the last inspection by the oil spill removal organization(s).

## A.3.6.2 Personnel

| RCRA (40 CFR part 264, Subpart D, 40 CFR Part 265, Subpart D, and 40 CFR 279.52 | EPA's Oil Pollution Prevention Regulation (40 CFR Part 112) | USCG-FRG (33 CFR Part 154) | DOT/RSPA-FRP (49 CFR part 194) |
|---|---|---|---|
|  | 112.20(h)(1)(v) 112.20(h)(3)(v) F1.3.4 | 1035(b)(3)(iv) |  |

### EPA's Oil Prevention Regulation

Section 1.3.4 lists the facility response personnel, including those employed by the facility and those under contract to the facility for response activities, the amount of time needed for personnel to respond, their responsibility in the case of an emergency, and their level of response training. Three different forms are included in this section. The Emergency Response Personnel List *shall* be composed of all personnel employed by the facility whose duties involve responding to emergencies, including oil discharges, even when they are not physically present at the site. An example of this type of person would be the Building Engineer-in-Charge or Plant Fire Chief. The second form is a list of the Emergency Response Contractors (both primary and secondary) retained by the facility. Any changes in contractor status **must** be reflected in updates to the response plan. Evidence of contracts with response contractors *shall* be included in this section so that the availability of resources can be verified. The last form is the Facility Response Team List, which *shall* be composed of both emergency response personnel (referenced by job title/position) and emergency response contractors, included in one of the two lists described above, that will respond immediately upon discovery of an oil discharge or other emergency (i.e., the first people to respond). These are to be persons normally on the facility premises or primary response contractors. Examples of these personnel would be the Facility Hazardous Materials (HAZMAT) Spill Team 1, Facility Fire Engine Company 1, Production Supervisor, or Transfer Supervisor. Company personnel **must** be able to respond immediately and adequately if contractor support is not available.

## USCG-FRP

This subsection **must** identify the oil spill removal organizations and the spill management team to:
Be capable of providing the following response resources:

(1) Equipment and supplies to meet the requirements of Secs. 154.1045, 154.1047 or subparts H or I of this part, as appropriate; and
(2) Trained personnel necessary to continue operation of the equipment and staff of the oil spill removal organization and spill management team for the first 7 days of the response.

This section **must** include job descriptions for each spill management team member within the organizational structure described in paragraph (b)(3)(iii) of this section. These job descriptions should include the responsibilities and duties of each spill management team member in a response action.

For mobile facilities that operate in more than one COTP zone, the plan **must** identify the oil spill removal organization and the spill management team in the applicable geographic-specific appendix. The oil spill removal organization(s) and the spill management team discussed in paragraph (b)(3)(iv)(A) of this section **must** be included for each COTP zone in which the facility will handle, store, or transport oil in bulk.

## A.3.6.3 Response Equipment

| RCRA (40 CFR part 264, Subpart D, 40 CFR Part 265, Subpart D, and 40 CFR 279.52 | EPA's Oil Pollution Prevention Regulation (40 CFR Part 112) | USCG-FRG (33 CFR Part 154) | OSHA HAZWOPER (29 CFR 1910.120) |
|---|---|---|---|
| 264.52(e) 265.52(e) 279.52(b)(2)(v) | 112.20(h)(1)(iv) 112.20(h)(3)(vi) F1.3.2 F1.7.1 | 1035(b)(2)(ii) 1035(b)(4)(iii) 1035(e)(3) Appendix C | (l)(2)(xi) (p)(8)(ii)(K) (q)(2)(xi) |

### RCRA

The plan **must** include a list of all emergency equipment at the facility (such as fire extinguishing systems, spill control equipment, communications and alarm systems (internal and external), and decontamination equipment), where this equipment is required. This list **must** be kept up to date. In addition, the plan **must** include the location and a physical description of each item on the list, and a brief outline of its capabilities.

### EPA's Oil Prevention Regulation

Section 1.3.2 provides a description of the facility's list of emergency response equipment and location of the response equipment.

When appropriate, the amount of oil that emergency response equipment can handle and any limitations (e.g., launching sites) **must** be described.

*Response Resources for Small, Medium, and Worst Case Discharges*

Once the discharge scenarios have been identified in section 1.5 of the response plan, the facility owner or operator *shall* identify and describe implementation of the response actions. The facility owner or operator *shall* demonstrate accessibility to the proper response personnel and equipment to effectively respond to all of the identified discharge scenarios. The determination and demonstration of adequate response capability are presented in Appendix E to this part.

In addition, steps to expedite the cleanup of oil discharges **must** be discussed. At a minimum, the following items **must** be addressed:

(1) Emergency plans for spill response;

(2) Additional response training;

(3) Additional contracted help;

(4) Access to additional response equipment/experts; and

(5) Ability to implement the plan including response training and practice drills.

## USCG-FRP

Appendix C to Part 154—Guidelines for Determining and Evaluating Required Response Resources for Facility Response Planss

1. Purpose

The purpose of this appendix is to describe the procedures for identifying response resources to meet the requirements of subpart F of this part. These guidelines will be used by the facility owner or operator in preparing the response plan and by the Captain of the Port (COTP) when reviewing them. Response resources identified in subparts H and I of this part should be selected using the guidelines in section 2 and Table 1 of this appendix.

## 2. Equipment Operability and Readiness

2.1 All equipment identified in a response plan **must** be designed to operate in the conditions expected in the facility's geographic area.

These conditions vary widely based on location and season. Therefore, it is difficult to identify a single stockpile of response equipment that will function effectively in each geographic location.

2.2 Facilities handling, storing, or transporting oil in more than one operating environment as indicated in Table 1 of this appendix **must** identify equipment capable of successfully functioning in each operating environment.

2.3 When identifying equipment for response plan credit, a facility owner or operator **must** consider the inherent limitations in the operability of equipment components and response systems. The criteria in Table 1 of this appendix should be used for evaluating the operability in a given environment. These criteria reflect the general conditions in certain operating areas.

2.3.1 The Coast Guard may require documentation that the boom identified in a response plan meets the criteria in Table 1. Absent acceptable documentation, the Coast Guard may require that the boom be tested to demonstrate that it meets the criteria in Table 1. Testing **must** be in accordance with ASTM F 715 (incorporated by reference, see Sec. 154.106), or other tests approved by the Coast Guard.

2.4 Table 1 of this appendix lists criteria for oil recovery devices and boom. All other equipment necessary to sustain or support response operations in the specified operating environment **must** be designed to function in the same conditions. For example, boats which deploy or support skimmers or boom **must** be capable of being safely operated in the significant wave heights listed for the applicable operating environment.

2.5 A facility owner or operator **must** refer to the applicable local contingency plan or ACP, as appropriate, to determine if ice, debris, and weather-related visibility are significant factors in evaluating the operability of equipment. The local contingency plan or ACP will also identify the average temperature ranges expected in the facility's operating area. All equipment identified in a response plan **must** be designed to operate within those conditions or ranges.

2.6 The requirements of subparts F, G, H and I of this part establish response resource mobilization and response times. The distance of the facility from the storage location of the response resources **must** be used to determine whether the resources can arrive on scene within the stated time. A facility owner or operator *shall* include the time for notification, mobilization, and travel time of response resources identified to meet the maximum most probable discharge and Tier 1 worst case discharge response time requirements. For subparts F and G, tier 2 and 3 response resources **must** be notified and mobilized as necessary to meet the requirements for arrival on scene in accordance with Secs. 154.1045 or 154.1047 of subpart F, or Sec. 154.1135 of subpart G, as appropriate. An on water speed of 5 knots and a land speed of 35 miles per hour is assumed unless the facility owner or operator can demonstrate otherwise.

2.7 For subparts F and G, in identifying equipment, the facility owner or operator *shall* list the storage location, quantity, and manufacturer's make and model. For oil recovery devices, the effective daily recovery capacity, as determined using section 6 of this appendix **must** be included. For boom, the overall boom height (draft plus freeboard) should be included. A facility owner or operator is responsible for ensuring that identified boom has compatible connectors.

2.8 For subparts H and I, in identifying equipment, the facility owner or operator *shall* list the storage location, quantity, and manufacturer's make and model. For boom, the overall boom height (draft plus freeboard) should be included. A facility owner or operator is responsible for ensuring that identified boom has compatible connectors.

3. Determining Response Resources Required for the Average Most Probable Discharge

3.1 A facility owner or operator *shall* identify sufficient response resources available, through contract or other approved means as described in Sec. 154.1028(a), to respond to the average most probable discharge. The equipment **must** be designed to function in the operating environment at the point of expected use.

3.2 The response resources **must** include:

3.2.1 1,000 feet of containment boom or two times the length of the largest vessel that regularly conducts oil transfers to or from the facility, whichever is greater, and a means deploying it available at the spill site within 1 hour of the discovery of a spill.

3.2.2 Oil recovery devices with an effective daily recovery capacity equal to the amount of oil discharged in an average most probable discharge or greater available at the facility within 2 hours of the detection of an oil discharge.

3.2.3 Oil storage capacity for recovered oily material indicated in section 9.2 of this appendix.

4. Determining Response Resources Required for the Maximum Most Probable Discharge

4.1 A facility owner or operator *shall* identify sufficient response resources available, by contract or other approved means as described in Sec. 154.1028(a), to respond to discharges up to the maximum most probable discharge volume for that facility. This will require response resources capable of containing and collecting up to 1,200 barrels of oil or 10 percent of the worst case discharge, whichever is less. All equipment identified **must** be designed to operate in the applicable operating environment specified in Table 1 of this appendix.

4.2 Oil recovery devices identified to meet the applicable maximum most probable discharge volume planning criteria **must** be located such that they arrive on scene within 6 hours in higher volume port areas (as defined in 154.1020) and the Great Lakes and within 12 hours in all other areas.

4.3 Because rapid control, containment, and removal of oil is critical to reduce spill impact, the effective daily recovery capacity for oil recovery devices **must** equal 50 percent of the planning volume applicable for the facility as determined in section 4.1 of this appendix. The effective daily recovery capacity for oil recovery devices identified in the plan **must** be determined using the criteria in section 6 of this appendix.

4.4 In addition to oil recovery capacity, the plan **must** identify sufficient quantities of containment boom available, by contract or other approved means as described in Sec. 154.1028(a), to arrive within the required response times for oil collection and containment and for protection of fish and wildlife and sensitive environments. While the regulation does not set required quantities of boom for oil collection and containment, the response plan **must** identify and ensure, by contract or other approved means as described in Sec. 154.1028(a), the availability of the boom identified in the plan for this purpose.

4.5 The plan **must** indicate the availability of temporary storage capacity to meet the guidelines of section 9.2 of this appendix. If available storage capacity is insufficient to meet this level, then the effective daily recovery capacity **must** be derated to the limits of the available storage capacity.

4.6 The following is an example of a maximum most probable discharge volume planning calculation for equipment identification in a higher volume port area: The facility's worst case discharge volume is 20,000 barrels. Ten percent of this is 2,000 barrels. Since this is greater than 1,200 barrels, 1,200 barrels is used as the planning volume. The effective daily recovery capacity **must** be 50 percent of this, or 600 barrels per day. The ability of oil recovery devices to meet this capacity will be calculated using the procedures in section 6 of this appendix. Temporary storage capacity available on scene **must** equal twice the daily recovery rate as indicated in section 9 of this appendix, or 1,200 barrels per day. This is the information the facility owner or operator will use to identify and ensure the availability of, through contract or other approved means as described in Sec. 154.1028(a), the required response resources. The facility owner will also need to identify how much boom is available for use.

5. Determining Response Resources Required for the Worst Case Discharge to the Maximum Extent Practicable

5.1 A facility owner or operator *shall* identify and ensure availability of, by contract or other approved means, as described in Sec. 154.1028(a), sufficient response resources to respond to the worst case discharge of oil to the maximum extent practicable. Section 7 of this appendix describes the method to determine the required response resources.

5.2 Oil spill response resources identified in the response plan and available through contract or other approved means, as described in Sec. 154.1028(a), to meet the applicable worst case discharge planning volume **must** be located such that they can arrive at the scene of a discharge within the times specified for the applicable response tiers listed in Sec. 154.1045.

5.3 The effective daily recovery capacity for oil recovery devices identified in a response plan **must** be determined using the criteria in section 6 of this appendix. A facility owner or operator *shall* identify the storage locations of all response resources that **must** be used to fulfill the requirements for each tier. The owner or operator of a facility whose required daily recovery capacity exceeds the applicable response capability caps in Table 5 of this appendix *shall* identify sources of additional equipment, their locations, and the arrangements made to obtain this equipment during a response. The owner or operator of a facility whose calculated planning volume exceeds the applicable contracting caps in Table 5 *shall* identify sources of additional equipment equal to twice the cap listed in Tiers 1, 2, and 3 or the amount necessary to reach the calculated planning volume, whichever is lower. The resources identified above the cap **must** be capable of arriving on scene not later than the Tiers 1, 2, and 3 response times in Sec. 154.1045. No contract is required. While general listings of available response equipment may be used to identify additional sources, a response plan **must** identify the specific sources, locations, and quantities of equipment that a facility owner or operator has considered in his or her planning. When listing Coast Guard classified oil spill removal organization(s) which have sufficient removal capacity to recover the volume above the response capability cap for the specific facility, as specified in Table 5 of this appendix, it is not necessary to list specific quantities of equipment.

5.4 A facility owner or operator *shall* identify the availability of temporary storage capacity to meet the requirements of section 9.2 of this appendix. If available storage capacity is insufficient to meet this requirement, then the effective daily recovery capacity **must** be derated to the limits of the available storage capacity.

5.5 When selecting response resources necessary to meet the response plan requirements, the facility owner or operator **must** ensure that a portion of those resources are capable of being used in close-to-shore response activities in *shall*ow water. The following percentages of the on-water response equipment identified for the applicable geographic area **must** be capable of operating in waters of 6 feet or less depth:

(i) Offshore—10 percentt

(ii) Nearshore/inland/Great Lakes/rivers and canals—20 percent..

5.6 In addition to oil spill recovery devices, a facility owner or operator *shall* identify sufficient quantities of boom that are available, by contract or other approved means as described in Sec. 154.1028(a), to arrive on scene within the required response times for oil containment and collection. The specific quantity of boom required for collection and containment will depend on the specific recovery equipment and strategies employed. A facility owner or operator *shall* also identify sufficient quantities of oil containment boom to protect fish and wildlife and sensitive environments for the number of days and geographic areas specified in Table 2. Sections 154.1035(b)(4)(iii) and 154.1040(a), as appropriate, *shall* be used to determine the amount of containment boom required, through contract or other approved means as described in Sec. 154.1028(a), to protect fish and wildlife and sensitive environments.

5.7 A facility owner or operator **must** also identify, through contract or other approved means as described in Sec. 154.1028(a), the availability of an oil spill removal organization capable of responding to a shoreline cleanup operation involving the calculated volume of oil and emulsified oil that might impact the affected shoreline. The volume of oil that **must** be planned for is calculated through the application of factors contained in Tables 2 and 3. The volume calculated from these tables is intended to assist the facility owner or operator in identifying a contractor with sufficient resources and expertise. This planning volume is not used explicitly to determine a required amount of equipment and personnel.

## 6. Determining Effective Daily Recovery Capacity for Oil Recovery Devices

6.1 Oil recovery devices identified by a facility owner or operator **must** be identified by manufacturer, model, and effective daily recovery capacity. These rates **must** be used to determine whether there is sufficient capacity to meet the applicable planning criteria for the average most probable discharge, maximum most probable discharge, and worst case discharge to the maximum extent practicable.

6.2 For the purpose of determining the effective daily recovery capacity of oil recovery devices, the formula listed in section 6.2.1 of this appendix will be used. This method considers potential limitations due to available daylight, weather, sea state, and percentage of emulsified oil in the recovered material. The Coast Guard may assign a lower efficiency factor to equipment listed in a response plan if it determines that such a reduction is warranted.

6.2.1 The following formula **must** be used to calculate the effective daily recovery capacity:

R=T x 24 hours x E

R=Effective daily recovery capacity
T=Throughout rate in barrels per hour (nameplate capacity)
E=20 percent Efficiency factor (or lower factor as determined by Coast Guard)

6.2.2 For those devices in which the pump limits the throughput of liquid, throughput rate will be calculated using the pump capacity.

6.2.3 For belt or mop type devices, the throughput rate will be calculated using the speed of the belt or mop through the device, assumed thickness of oil adhering to or collected by the device, and surface area of the belt or mop. For purposes of this calculation, the assumed thickness of oil will be 1/4 inch.

6.2.4 Facility owners or operators including oil recovery devices whose throughput is not measurable using a pump capacity or belt/mop speed may provide information to support an alternative method of calculation. This information **must** be submitted following the procedures in paragraph 6.3.2 of this appendix.

6.3 As an alternative to 6.2, a facility owner or operator may submit adequate evidence that a different effective daily recovery capacity should be applied for a specific oil recovery device. Adequate evidence is actual verified performance data in spill conditions or tests using ASTM F 631 (incorporated by reference, see Sec. 154.106), or an equivalent test approved by the Coast Guard.

6.3.1 The following formula **must** be used to calculate the effective daily recovery capacity under this alternative:

R=D x U

R=Effective daily recovery capacity
D=Average Oil Recovery Rate in barrels per hour (Item 26 in ASTM F 808; Item 13.2.16 in ASTM F 631; or actual performance data)
U=Hours per day that a facility owner or operator can document capability to operate equipment under spill conditions. Ten hours per day **must** be used unless a facility owner or operator can demonstrate that the recovery operation can be sustained for longer periods.

6.3.2 A facility owner or operator proposing a different effective daily recovery rate for use in a response plan *shall* provide data for the oil recovery devices listed. The following is an example of these calculations:

A weir skimmer identified in a response plan has a manufacturer's rated throughput at the pump of 267 gallons per minute (gpm).

267 gpm=381 barrels per hour
R=381 x 24 x .2=1829 barrels per day

After testing using ASTM procedures, the skimmer's oil recovery rate is determined to be 220 gpm. The facility owner of operator identifies sufficient response resources available to support operations 12 hours per day.

220 gpm=314 barrels per hour
R=314 x 12=3768 barrels per day

The facility owner or operator will be able to use the higher rate if sufficient temporary oil storage capacity is available.

Determinations of alternative efficiency factors under paragraph 6.2 or alternative effective daily recovery capacities under paragraph 6.3 of this appendix will be made by Commandant, (G-MOR), Coast Guard Headquarters, 2100 Second Street SW., Washington, DC 20593. Response contractors or equipment manufacturers may submit required information on behalf of multiple facility owners or operators directly in lieu of including the request with the response plan submission.

7. Calculating the Worst Case Discharge Planning Volumes

7.1 The facility owner or operator *shall* plan for a response to a facility's worst case discharge. The planning for on-water recovery **must** take into account a loss of some oil to the environment due to evaporative and natural dissipation, potential increases in volume due to emulsification, and the potential for deposit of some oil on the shoreline.

7.2 The following procedures **must** be used to calculate the planning volume used by a facility owner or operator for determining required on water recovery capacity:

7.2.1 The following **must** be determined: The worst case discharge volume of oil in the facility; the appropriate group(s) for the type of oil handled, stored, or transported at the facility (non-persistent (Group I) or persistent (Groups II, III, or IV)); and the facility's specific operating area. Facilities which handle, store, or transport oil from different petroleum oil groups **must** calculate each group separately. This information is to be used with Table 2 of this appendix to determine the percentages of the total volume to be used for removal capacity planning. This table divides the volume into three categories: Oil lost to the environment; oil deposited on the shoreline; and oil available for on-water recovery.

7.2.2 The on-water oil recovery volume **must** be adjusted using the appropriate emulsification factor found in Table 3 of this appendix.

Facilities which handle, store, or transport oil from different petroleum groups **must** assume that the oil group resulting in the largest on-water recovery volume will be stored in the tank or tanks identified as constituting the worst case discharge.

7.2.3 The adjusted volume is multiplied by the on-water oil recovery resource mobilization favor found in Table 4 of this appendix from the appropriate operating area and response tier to determine the total on-water oil recovery capacity in barrels per day that **must** be identified or contracted for to arrive on-scene with the applicable time for each response tier. Three tiers are specified. For higher volume port areas, the contracted tiers of resources **must** be located such that they can arrive on scene within 6, 30, and 54 hours of the discovery of an oil discharge. For all other river, inland, nearshore, offshore areas, and the Great Lakes, these tiers are 12, 36, and 60 hours.

7.2.4 The resulting on-water recovery capacity in barrels per day for each tier **must** be used to identify response resources necessary to sustain operations in the applicable operating area. The equipment **must** be capable of sustaining operations for the time period specified in Table 2 of this appendix. The facility owner or operator **must** identify and ensure the availability, through contract or other approved means as described in Sec.154.1028 (a), of sufficient oil spill recovery devices to provide the effective daily recovery oil recovery capacity required.

If the required capacity exceeds the applicable cap specified in Table 5 of this appendix, then a facility owner or operator *shall* ensure, by contract or other approved means as described in Sec. 154.1028(a), only for the quantity of resources required to meet the cap, but *shall* identify sources of additional resources as indicated in Sec. 154.1045(m). The owner or operator of a facility whose planning volume exceeds the cap for 1993 **must** make arrangements to identify and ensure the availability, through contract or other approved means as described in Sec. 154.1028 (a), of the additional capacity in 1998 or 2003, as appropriate. For a facility that handles, stores, or transports multiple groups of oil, the required effective daily recovery capacity for each group is calculated before applying the cap.

7.3 The following procedures **must** be used to calculate the planning volume for identifying shoreline cleanup capacity:

7.3.1 The following **must** be determined: The worst case discharge volume of oil for the facility; the appropriate group(s) for the type of oil handled, stored, or transported at the facility (non-persistent (Group I) or persistent (Groups II, III, or IV)); and the operating area(s) in which the facility operates. For a facility storing oil from different groups, each group **must** be calculated separately. Using this information, Table 2 of this appendix **must** be used to determine the percentages of the total planning volume to be used for shoreline cleanup resource planning.

7.3.2 The shoreline cleanup planning volume **must** be adjusted to reflect an emulsification factor using the same procedure as described in section 7.2.2.

7.3.3 The resulting volume will be used to identify an oil spill removal organization with the appropriate shoreline cleanup capability.

7.3.4 The following is an example of the procedure described above: A facility receives oil from barges via a dock located on a bay and transported by piping to storage tanks. The facility handles Number 6 oil (specific gravity .96) and stores the oil in tanks where it is held prior to being burned in an electric generating plant. The MTR segment of the facility has six 18-inch diameter pipelines running one mile from the dock-side manifold to several storage tanks which are located in the non-transportation-related portion of the facility. Although the facility piping has a normal working pressure of 100 pounds per square inch, the piping has a maximum allowable working pressure (MAWP) of 150 pounds per square inch. At MAWP, the pumping system can move 10,000 barrels (bbls) of Number 6 oil every hour through each pipeline. The facility has a roving watchman who is required to drive the length of the piping every 2 hours when the facility is receiving oil from a barge. The facility operator estimates that it will take approximately 10 minutes to secure pumping operations when a discharge is discovered.

Using the definition of worst case discharge provided in Sec. 154.1029(b)(ii), the following calculation is provided:

Bbls.

2 hrs + 0.17 hour x 10,000 bbls per hour.................. 21,700
Piping volume = 37,322 ft \3\ <divide> 5.6 ft \3\/bbl......... +6,664

Discharge volume per pipe................................... 28,364

Number of pipelines........................................... x 6

Worst case discharge from MTR facility............... 170,184

To calculate the planning volumes for onshore recovery:

Worst case discharge: 170,184 bbls. Group IV oil
Emulsification factor (from Table 3): 1.4
Operating Area impacted: Inland
Planned percent oil onshore recovery (from Table 2): Inland 70%
Planning volumes for onshore recovery: Inland 170,184 x .7 x 1.4 =
166,780 bbls.

Conclusion: The facility owner or operator **must** contract with a response resource capable of managing a 166,780 barrel shoreline cleanup.
To calculate the planning volumes for on-water recovery:

Worst case discharge: 170,184 bbls. Group IV oil
Emulsification factor (from Table 3): 1.4
Operating Area impacted: Inland
Planned percent oil on-water recovery (from Table 2): Inland 50%
Planning volumes for on-water recovery: Inland 170,184 x .5 x 1.4 =
119,128 bbls.

To determine the required resources for on-water recovery for each tier, use the mobilization factors from Table 4:

|  | Tier 1 | Tier 2 | Tier 3 |
|---|---|---|---|
| Inland = 119,128 bbls | x.15 | x.25 | x. 40 |
| Barrels per day(pbd) | 17,869 | 29,782 | 47,652 |

Conclusion: Since the requirements for all tiers for inland exceed the caps, the facility owner will only need to contract for 10,000 bpd for Tier

1, 20,000 bpd for Tier 2, and 40,000 bpd for Tier 3. Sources for the bpd on-water recovery resources above the caps for all three

Tiers need only be identified in the response plan.

Twenty percent of the capability for Inland, for all tiers, **must** be capable of operating in water with a depth of 6 feet or less.

The facility owner or operator will also be required to identify or ensure, by contract or other approved means as described in Sec. 154.1028(a), sufficient response resources required under Secs. 154.1035(b) (4) and 154.1045(k) to protect fish and wildlife and sensitive environments identified in the response plan for the worst case discharge from the facility.

The COTP has the discretion to accept that a facility can operate only a limited number of the total pipelines at a dock at a time. In those circumstances, the worst case discharge **must** include the drainage volume from the piping normally not in use in addition to the drainage volume and volume of oil discharged during discovery and shut down of the oil discharge from the operating piping.

## 8. Determining the Availability of Alternative Response Methods

8.1 Response plans for facilities that handle, store, or transport Groups II or III persistent oils that operate in an area with year-round preapproval for dispersant use may receive credit for up to 25 percent of their required on-water recovery capacity for 1993 if the availability of these resources is ensured by contract or other approved means as described in Sec. 154.1028(a). For response plan credit, these resources **must** be capable of being on-scene within 12 hours of a discharge.

8.2 To receive credit against any required on-water recover capacity a response plan **must** identify the locations of dispersant stockpiles, methods of shipping to a staging area, and appropriate aircraft, vessels, or facilities to apply the dispersant and monitor its effectiveness at the scene of an oil discharge.

8.2.1 Sufficient volumes of dispersants **must** be available to treat the oil at the dosage rate recommended by the dispersant manufacturer. Dispersants identified in a response plan **must** be on the NCP Product Schedule that is maintained by the Environmental Protection Agency. (Some states have a list of approved dispersants and within state waters only they can be used.)

8.2.2 Dispersant application equipment identified in a response plan for credit **must** be located where it can be mobilized to shoreside staging areas to meet the time requirements in section 8.1 of this appendix. Sufficient equipment capacity and sources of appropriate dispersants should be identified to sustain dispersant application operations for at least 3 days.

8.2.3 Credit against on-water recovery capacity in preapproved areas will be based on the ability to treat oil at a rate equivalent to this credit. For example, a 2,500 barrel credit against the Tier 1 10,000 barrel on-water cap would require the facility owner or operator to demonstrate the ability to treat 2,500 barrel/day of oil at the manufacturers recommended dosage rate. Assuming a dosage rate of 10:1, the plan would need to show stockpiles and sources of 250 barrels of dispersants at a rate of 250 barrels per day and the ability to apply the dispersant at that daily rate for 3 days in the geographic area in which the facility is located. Similar data would need to be provided for any additional credit against Tier 2 and 3 resources.

8.3 In addition to the equipment and supplies required, a facility owner or operator *shall* identify a source of support to conduct the monitoring and post-use effectiveness evaluation required by applicable regional plans and ACPs.

Identification of the response resources for dispersant application does not imply that the use of this technique will be authorized. Actual authorization for use during a spill response will be governed by the provisions of the NCP and the applicable regional plan or ACP. A facility owner or operator who operates a facility in areas with year-round preapproval of dispersant can reduce the required on-water recovery capacity for 1993 up to 25 percent. A facility owner or operator may reduce the required on water recovery cap increase for 1998 and 2003 up to 50 percent by identifying pre-approved alternative response methods.

8.5 In addition to the credit identified above, a facility owner or operator that operates in a year-round area pre-approved for dispersant use may reduce their required on water recovery cap increase for 1998 and 2003 by up to 50 percent by identifying non-mechanical methods.

8.6 The use of in-situ burning as a non-mechanical response method is still being studied. Because limitations and uncertainties remain for the use of this method, it may not be used to reduce required oil recovery capacity in 1993.

## 9. Additional Equipment Necessary to Sustain Response Operations

9.1 A facility owner or operator is responsible for ensuring that sufficient numbers of trained personnel and boats, aerial spotting aircraft, containment boom, sorbent materials, boom anchoring materials, and other supplies are available to sustain response operations to completion. All such equipment **must** be suitable for use with the primary equipment identified in the response plan. A facility owner or operator is not required to list these response resources, but *shall* certify their availability.

9.2 A facility owner or operator *shall* evaluate the availability of adequate temporary storage capacity to sustain the effective daily recovery capacities from equipment identified in the plan. Because of the inefficiencies of oil spill recovery devices, response plans **must** identify daily storage capacity equivalent to twice the effective daily recovery rate required on scene. This temporary storage capacity may be reduced if a facility owner or operator can demonstrate by waste stream analysis that the efficiencies of the oil recovery devices, ability to decant waste, or the availability of alternative temporary storage or disposal locations will reduce the overall volume of oily material storage requirement.

9.3 A facility owner or operator *shall* ensure that his or her planning includes the capability to arrange for disposal of recovered oil products. Specific disposal procedures will be addressed in the applicable ACP.

TABLE 1.—RESPONSE RESOURCE OPERATING CRITERIA OIL RECOVERY DEVICES

| Operating environment | Significant wave height[1] | Sea State |
|---|---|---|
| Rivers and Canals | ≤1 Foot | 1 |
| Inland | ≤3 feet | 2 |
| Great Lakes | ≤4 feet | 2–3 |
| Ocean | ≤6 feet | 3–4 |

BOOM

| Boom property | Use | | | |
|---|---|---|---|---|
| | Rivers and canals | Inland | Great Lakes | Ocean |
| Significant Wave Height[1] | ≤1 | ≤3 | ≤4 | ≤6 |
| Sea State | 1 | 2 | 2–3 | 3–4 |
| Boom height—in. (draft plus freeboard) | 6–18 | 18–42 | 18–42 | ≤42 |
| Reserve Buoyancy to Weight Ratio | 2:1 | 2:1 | 2:1 | 3:1 to 4:1 |
| Total Tensile Strength—lbs. | 4,500 | 15–20,000 | 15–20,000 | ≤20,000 |
| Skirt Fabric Tensile Strength—lbs | 200 | 300 | 300 | 500 |
| Skirt Fabric Tear Strength—lbs | 100 | 100 | 100 | 125 |

[1] Oil recovery devices and boom must be at least capable of operating in wave heights up to and including the values listed in Table 1 for each operating environment.

TABLE 2.—REMOVAL CAPACITY PLANNING TABLE

| Spill location | Rivers and canals | | | Nearshore/inland Great Lakes | | | Offshore | | |
|---|---|---|---|---|---|---|---|---|---|
| Sustainability of on-water oil recovery | 3 Days | | | 4 Days | | | 6 Days | | |
| Oil group | % Natural dissipation | % Recovered floating oil | % Oil on shore | % Natural dissipation | % Recovered floating oil | % Oil on shore | % Natural dissipation | % Recovered floating oil | % Oil on shore |
| 1  Non-persistent oils | 80 | 10 | 10 | 80 | 20 | 10 | 95 | 5 | / |
| 2  Light crudes | 40 | 15 | 45 | 50 | 50 | 30 | 75 | 25 | 5 |
| 3  Medium crudes and fuels | 20 | 15 | 65 | 30 | 50 | 50 | 60 | 40 | 20 |
| 4  Heavy crudes and fuels | 5 | 20 | 75 | 10 | 50 | 70 | 50 | 40 | 30 |

TABLE 3.—EMULSIFICATION FACTORS FOR PETROLEUM OIL GROUPS

| | |
|---|---|
| Non-Persistent Oil: | |
| Group I | 1.0 |
| Persistent Oil: | |

TABLE 3.—EMULSIFICATION FACTORS FOR PETROLEUM OIL GROUPS—Continued

| | |
|---|---|
| Group II | 1.8 |
| Group III | 2.0 |
| Group IV | 1.4 |

TABLE 4.—ON WATER OIL RECOVERY
RESOURCE MOBILIZATION FACTORS

| Operating Area | Tier 1 | Tier 2 | Tier 3 |
|---|---|---|---|
| Rivers & Canals ................................. | .30 | .40 | .60 |
| Inland/Nearshore/Great Lakes ............ | .15 | .25 | .40 |

TABLE 4.—ON WATER OIL RECOVERY
RESOURCE MOBILIZATION FACTORS—Continued

| Operating Area | Tier 1 | Tier 2 | Tier 3 |
|---|---|---|---|
| Offshore ............................................ | .10 | .165 | .21 |

Note: These mobilization factors are for total response resources mobilized, not incremental response resources.

TABLE 5.—RESPONSE CAPABILITY CAPS BY OPERATING AREA

| | Tier 1 | Tier 2 | Tier 3 |
|---|---|---|---|
| **February 18, 1993:** | | | |
| All except rivers and canals, Great Lakes. | 10K bbls/day .................. | 20K bbls/day .................. | 40K bbls/day/ |
| Great Lakes .................................... | 5K bbls/day .................... | 10K bbls/day .................. | 20K bbls/day. |
| Rivers and canals ........................... | 1,500 bbls/day ............... | 3,000 bbls/day ............... | 6,000 bbls/day. |
| **February 18, 1998:** | | | |
| All except rivers and canals, Great Lakes. | 12.5K bbls/day ............... | 25K bbls/day ................. | 50K bbls/day. |
| Great Lakes .................................... | 6.35K bbls/day .............. | 12.3K bbls/day .............. | 25K bbls/day. |
| Rivers and canals ........................... | 1,875 bbls/day ............... | 3,750 bbls/day ............... | 7,500 bbls/day. |
| **February 18, 2003:** | | | |
| All except rivers and canals, Great Lakes. | TBD .............................. | TBD .............................. | TBD. |
| Great Lakes .................................... | TBD .............................. | TBD .............................. | TBD. |
| Rivers and canals ........................... | TBD .............................. | TBD .............................. | TBD. |

Note: The caps show cumulative overall effective daily recovery capacity, not incremental increases.
TBD=To be determined.

[CGD 91-036, 61 FR 7933, Feb. 29, 1996, as amended by CGD 96-026, 61 FR 33666, June 28, 1996; USCG-1999-5151, 64 FR 67175, Dec. 1, 1999; USCG-2000-7223, 65 FR 40058, June 29, 2000]

## OSHA HAZWOPER

PPE and emergency equipment

## A.3.6.4 Support Equipment

| RCRA (40 CFR part 264, Subpart D, 40 CFR Part 265, Subpart D, and 40 CFR 279.52 | EPA's Oil Pollution Prevention Regulation (40 CFR Part 112) | USCG-FRG (33 CFR Part 154) |
|---|---|---|
| 264.52(e) 265.52(e) 279.52(b)(2)(v) | F1.3.2 F1.7.1 | 1035(e)(3) |

## RCRA

The plan **must** include a list of all emergency equipment at the facility (such as fire extinguishing systems, spill control equipment, communications and alarm systems (internal and external), and decontamination equipment), where this equipment is required. This list **must** be kept up to date. In addition, the plan **must** include the location and a physical description of each item on the list, and a brief outline of its capabilities.

## EPA's Oil Prevention Regulation

Section 1.3.2 provides a description of the facility's list of emergency response equipment and location of the response equipment.

When appropriate, the amount of oil that emergency response equipment can handle and any limitations (e.g., launching sites) **must** be described.

### *Response Resources for Small, Medium, and Worst Case Discharges*

Once the discharge scenarios have been identified in section 1.5 of the response plan, the facility owner or operator *shall* identify and describe implementation of the response actions. The facility owner or operator *shall* demonstrate accessibility to the proper response personnel and equipment to effectively respond to all of the identified discharge scenarios. The determination and demonstration of adequate response capability are presented in Appendix E to this part.

In addition, steps to expedite the cleanup of oil discharges **must** be discussed. At a minimum, the following items **must** be addressed:
(1) Emergency plans for spill response;
(2) Additional response training;
(3) Additional contracted help;
(4) Access to additional response equipment/experts; and
(5) Ability to implement the plan including response training and practice drills.

## A.3.6.5 Contracting

| EPA's Oil Pollution Prevention Regulation (40 CFR Part 112) | USCG-FRG (33 CFR Part 154) | DOT/RSPA-FRP (49 CFR part 194) |
|---|---|---|
| 112.20(h)(3)(ii) | 1028(a)(1) 1035(e)(3) | 194.115 |

### EPA's Oil Prevention Regulation

Evidence of contracts or other approved means for ensuring the availability of such personnel and equipment.

### USCG-FRP

*Equipment list and records.*

This appendix **must** include the information specified in this paragraph.

The appendix **must** contain a list of equipment and facility personnel required to respond to an average most probable discharge, as defined in Sec. 154.1020. The appendix **must** also list the location of the equipment.

The appendix **must** contain a detailed listing of all the major equipment identified in the plan as belonging to an oil spill removal organization(s) that is available, by contract or other approved means as described in Sec. 154.1028(a), to respond to a maximum most probable or worst case discharge, as defined in Sec. 154.1020. The detailed listing of all major equipment may be located in a separate document referenced by the plan. Either the appendix or the separate document referenced in the plan **must** provide the location of the major response equipment.

It is not necessary to list response equipment from oil spill removal organization(s) when the organization has been classified by the Coast

Guard and their capacity has been determined to equal or exceed the response capability needed by the facility. For oil spill removal organization(s) classified by the Coast Guard, the classification **must** be noted in this section of the plan. When it is necessary for the appendix to contain a listing of response equipment, it *shall* include all of the following items that are identified in the response plan:

Skimmers; booms; dispersant application, in-situ burning, bioremediation equipment and supplies, and other equipment used to apply other chemical agents on the NCP Product Schedule (if applicable); communications, firefighting, and beach cleaning equipment; boats and motors; disposal and storage equipment; and heavy equipment. The list **must** include for each piece of equipment—

(A) The type, make, model, and year of manufacture listed on the name-plate of the equipment;

(B) For oil recovery devices, the effective daily recovery rate, as determined using section 6 of Appendix C of this part;

(C) For containment boom, the overall boom height (draft and freeboard) and type of end connectors;

(D) The spill scenario in which the equipment will be used for or which it is contracted;

(E) The total daily capacity for storage and disposal of recovered oil;

(F) For communication equipment, the type and amount of equipment intended for use during response activities. Where applicable, the primary and secondary radio frequencies **must** be specified.

(G) Location of the equipment; and

(H) The date of the last inspection by the oil spill removal organization(s).

## DOT/RSPA-FRP

*Response resources.*

Each operator *shall* identify and ensure, by contract or other approved means, the resources necessary to remove, to the maximum extent practicable, a worst case discharge and to mitigate or prevent a substantial threat of a worst case discharge.

An operator *shall* identify in the response plan the response resources which are available to respond within the time specified, after discovery of a worst case discharge, or to mitigate the substantial threat of such a discharge, as follows:

## A.3.6.6 Claims Procedures

The person or persons responsible for discharges or releases are liable for costs of cleanup. The OSC *shall* attempt to have the party responsible for the discharge or release voluntarily assume responsibility for containment, removal, and disposal operations. If the OSC determines that the responsible party has caused the discharge of oil or release of hazardous substances, he/she may initiate appropriate response actions established by OPA, CWA, or CERCLA. Action will be initiated by the agency administering the funding mechanism to recover such expenditures from the party responsible for the discharge, if known. The OSC may also issue an Administrative Order, either by consent or unilaterally, to require financially viable responsible parties to conduct the removal action.

Until new guidance is published, all incidents requiring funding **must** be screened by category:

(a) CWA Section 311(k) for oil only, and
(b) CERCLA for any release or threat of release of a hazardous material as defined by CERCLA.

A U.S. EPA and USCG Headquarters agreement states that response to any potentially hazardous oil and hazardous materials mixture *shall* be CERCLA-funded. This section addresses U.S. EPA and State access to OPA and CERCLA funding. USCG procedures can be found in USCG ACPs.

| RCRA (40 CFR part 264, Subpart D, 40 CFR Part 265, Subpart D, and 40 CFR 279.52 | EPA's Oil Pollution Prevention Regulation (40 CFR Part 112) | USCG-FRG (33 CFR Part 154) | DOT/RSPA-FRP (49 CFR part 194) | OSHA Emergency Action Plans (29 CFR 1910.38(a)) and Process Safety (29 CFR 1910.119) | OSHA HAZWOPER (29 CFR 1910.120) | CAA RMP (40 CFR part 68) |
|---|---|---|---|---|---|---|
| | | | | | | |

## A.3.6.7 Cost Documentation

| RCRA (40 CFR part 264, Subpart D, 40 CFR Part 265, Subpart D, and 40 CFR 279.52 | EPA's Oil Pollution Prevention Regulation (40 CFR Part 112) | USCG-FRG (33 CFR Part 154) | DOT/RSPA-FRP (49 CFR part 194) | OSHA Emergency Action Plans (29 CFR 1910.38(a)) and Process Safety (29 CFR 1910.119) | OSHA HAZWOP ER (29 CFR 1910.120) | CAA RMP (40 CFR part 68) |
|---|---|---|---|---|---|---|
| | | | | | | |

The OSC in charge at the scene of a release may be from any one of several agencies. It is necessary, therefore, to establish uniform procedures for notification of counsel and for collection of samples and information consistent with the several phases in Federal response situations. Necessary information and sample collection **must** be performed at the proper times during Federal involvement in a spill for the purpose of later use in identifying the party responsible for cost recovery.

Time is of great importance, as wind, tide, and current may disperse or remove the evidence and witnesses may no longer be available. Thus, during the response phases, the OSC **must** take the necessary action to ensure that information, records, and samples adequate for legal and research purposes are obtained and safeguarded for future use.

Section 300.335 of the NCP outlines the types of funds which may be available to address certain oil and hazardous substances discharges. For releases of oil or a hazardous substance, pollutant, or contaminant, the following provisions apply:

(a) During all phases of response, the lead agency *shall* complete and maintain documentation to support all actions taken under the ACP and to form the basis for cost recovery. In general, documentation *shall* be sufficient to provide the source and circumstances of release; identity of responsible parties; response action taken; accurate accounting of Federal, State, or private party costs incurred for response actions; and impacts and potential impacts to public health and welfare and the environment. Where applicable, documentation *shall* state when the NRC received notification of release of a reportable quantity.

(b) The information and reports obtained by the lead agency for OSLTF financed response actions *shall*, as appropriate, be transmitted to the NPFC. Copies can then be forwarded to the NRT, members of the RRT, and others as appropriate.

# Annex 4.0: Incident Documentation

This annex should describe the company's procedures for conducting a follow-up investigation of the cause of the accident, including coordination with federal, State, and local officials. This annex should also contain an accounting of incidents that have occurred at the facility, including information on cause, amount released, resources impacted, injuries, response actions, etc. This annex should also include information that may be required to prove that the facility met its legal notification requirements with respect to a given incident, such as a signed record of initial notifications and certified copies of written follow-up reports submitted after a response.

| OSHA Emergency Action Plans (29 CFR 1910.38(a)) and Process Safety (29 CFR 1910.119) | OSHA HAZWOPER (29 CFR 1910.120) |
|---|---|
| 38(a)(2)(iii)<br>119(e)(3)(ii) | (1)(2)(x)<br>(p)(8)(ii)(J)<br>(q)(2)(x) |

## OSHA Emergency Action Plans

Procedures to account for all employees after emergency evacuation have been completed.

## OSHA Process Safety

The identification of any previous incident which had a likely potential for catastrophic consequences in the workplace.

## OSHA HAZWOPER

Critique of response and follow-up.

## A.4.1 Post-Accident

| RCRA (40 CFR part 264, Subpart D, 40 CFR Part 265, Subpart D, and 40 CFR 279.52 | EPA's Oil Pollution Prevention Regulation (40 CFR Part 112) | USCG-FRG (33 CFR Part 154) | DOT/RSP A-FRP (49 CFR part 194) | OSHA Emergency Action Plans (29 CFR 1910.38(a)) and Process Safety (29 CFR 1910.119) | OSHA HAZWOPER (29 CFR 1910.120) | CAA RMP (40 CFR part 68) |
|---|---|---|---|---|---|---|
| 264.56(j)<br>265.56(j)<br>279.52(b)(6)(ix) | | | | 119(m) | (l)(2)(x)<br>(p)(8)(ii)(J)<br>(q)(2)(x) | 68.60<br>68.81 |

## RCRA

The owner or operator **must** note in the operating record the time, date, and details of any incident that requires implementing the contingency plan. Within 15 days after the incident, he **must** submit a written report on the incident to the Regional Administrator. The report **must** include:

(1) Name, address, and telephone number of the owner or operator;

(2) Name, address, and telephone number of the facility;

(3) Date, time, and type of incident (e.g., fire, explosion);

(4) Name and quantity of material(s) involved;

(5) The extent of injuries, if any;

(6) An assessment of actual or potential hazards to human health or the environment, where this is applicable; and

(7) Estimated quantity and disposition of recovered material that resulted from the incident.

## OSHA Process Safety

*Incident investigation.*

The employer *shall* investigate each incident which resulted in, or could reasonably have resulted in a catastrophic release of highly hazardous chemical in the workplace.

An incident investigation *shall* be initiated as promptly as possible, but not later than 48 hours following the incident.

An incident investigation team *shall* be established and consist of at least one person knowledgeable in the process involved, including a contract employee if the incident involved work of the contractor, and other persons with appropriate knowledge and experience to thoroughly investigate and analyze the incident.

A report *shall* be prepared at the conclusion of the investigation which includes at a minimum:
- Date of incident;
- Date investigation began;
- A description of the incident;
- The factors that contributed to the incident; and,
- Any recommendations resulting from the investigation.

The employer *shall* establish a system to promptly address and resolve the incident report findings and recommendations. Resolutions and corrective actions *shall* be documented.

The report *shall* be reviewed with all affected personnel whose job tasks are relevant to the incident findings including contract employees where applicable.

Incident investigation reports *shall* be retained for five years.

## OSHA HAZWOPER

Critique of response and follow-up

## CAA RMP

*Sec. 68.60 Incident investigation.*

The owner or operator *shall* investigate each incident which resulted in, or could reasonably have resulted in a catastrophic release.

An incident investigation *shall* be initiated as promptly as possible, but not later than 48 hours following the incident.

A summary *shall* be prepared at the conclusion of the investigation which includes at a minimum:

(1) Date of incident;
(2) Date investigation began;
(3) A description of the incident;
(4) The factors that contributed to the incident; and,
(5) Any recommendations resulting from the investigation.

The owner or operator *shall* promptly address and resolve the investigation findings and recommendations. Resolutions and corrective actions *shall* be documented.

The findings *shall* be reviewed with all affected personnel whose job tasks are affected by the findings.

Investigation summaries *shall* be retained for five years.

*Sec. 68.81 Incident investigation.*

The owner or operator *shall* investigate each incident which resulted in, or could reasonably have resulted in a catastrophic release of a regulated substance.

An incident investigation *shall* be initiated as promptly as possible, but not later than 48 hours following the incident.

**An incident investigation team *shall* be established and consist of at least one person knowledgeable in the process involved, including a contract employee if the incident involved work of the contractor, and other persons with appropriate knowledge and experience to thoroughly investigate and analyze the incident.**

A report *shall* be prepared at the conclusion of the investigation which includes at a minimum:

(1) Date of incident;

(2) Date investigation began;

(3) A description of the incident;

(4) The factors that contributed to the incident; and,

(5) Any recommendations resulting from the investigation.

The owner or operator *shall* establish a system to promptly address and resolve the incident report findings and recommendations.

Resolutions and corrective actions *shall* be documented.

The report *shall* be reviewed with all affected personnel whose job tasks are relevant to the incident findings including contract employees where applicable.

Incident investigation reports *shall* be retained for five years.

## A.4.2 Incident History

| RCRA (40 CFR part 264, Subpart D, 40 CFR Part 265, Subpart D, and 40 CFR 279.52 | EPA's Oil Pollution Prevention Regulation (40 CFR Part 112) | USCG-FRG (33 CFR Part 154) | DOT/RS PA-FRP (49 CFR part 194) | OSHA Emergency Action Plans (29 CFR 1910.38(a)) and Process Safety (29 CFR 1910.119) | OSHA HAZWOP ER (29 CFR 1910.120) | CAA RMP (40 CFR part 68) |
|---|---|---|---|---|---|---|
|  | 112.20(h)(4) F1.4.4 |  |  | 119(e)(3)(ii) |  | 68.42 |

### EPA's Oil Prevention Regulation

*Hazard evaluation.*

The response plan *shall* discuss the facility's known or reasonably identifiable history of discharges reportable under 40 CFR part 110 for the entire life of the facility and *shall* identify areas within the facility where discharges could occur and what the potential effects of the discharges would be on the affected environment. To assess the range of areas potentially affected, owners or operators *shall*, where appropriate, consider the distance calculated in paragraph (f) (1) (ii) of this section to determine whether a facility could, because of its location, reasonably be expected to cause substantial harm to the environment by discharging oil into or on the navigable waters or adjoining shorelines.

*Facility Reportable Oil Spill History*

Briefly describe the facility's reportable oil spill3 history for the entire life of the facility to the extent that such information is reasonably identifiable, including:

(1) Date of discharge(s);
(2) List of discharge causes;
(3) Material(s) discharged;
(4) Amount discharged in gallons;
(5) Amount of discharge that reached navigable waters, if applicable;
(6) Effectiveness and capacity of secondary containment;
(7) Clean-up actions taken;
(8) Steps taken to reduce possibility of recurrence;
(9) Total oil storage capacity of the tank(s) or impoundment(s) from which the material discharged;
(10) Enforcement actions;
(11) Effectiveness of monitoring equipment; and
(12) Description(s) of how each oil discharge was detected.

The information solicited in this section may be similar to requirements in 40 CFR 112.4(a). Any duplicate information required by Sec. 112.4(a) may be photocopied and inserted.

³ As described in 40 CFR part 110, reportable oil spills are those that: (a) violate applicable water quality standards, or (b) cause a film or sheen upon or discoloration of the surface of the water or adjoining shorelines or cause a sludge or emulsion to be deposited beneath the surface of the water or upon adjoining shorelines.

## OSHA Process Safety

The identification of any previous incident which had a likely potential for catastrophic consequences in the workplace.

## CAA RMP

*Five-year accident history.*

The owner or operator *shall* include in the five-year accident history all accidental releases from covered processes that resulted in deaths, injuries, or significant property damage on site, or known offsite deaths, injuries, evacuations, sheltering in place, property damage, or environmental damage.

Data required. For each accidental release included, the owner or operator *shall* report the following information:

(1) Date, time, and approximate duration of the release;
(2) Chemical(s) released;
(3) Estimated quantity released in pounds and, for mixtures containing regulated toxic substances, percentage concentration by weight of the released regulated toxic substance in the liquid mixture;
(4) Five- or six-digit NAICS code that most closely corresponds to the process;
(5) The type of release event and its source;
(6) Weather conditions, if known;
(7) On-site impacts;
(8) Known offsite impacts;

(9) Initiating event and contributing factors if known;

(10) Whether offsite responders were notified if known; and

(11) Operational or process changes that resulted from investigation of the release.

Level of accuracy. Numerical estimates may be provided to two significant digits.

# Annex 5.0: Training and Exercise/Drills

This annex should contain a description of the training and exercise program conducted at the facility as well as evidence (i.e., logs) that required training and exercises have been conducted on a regular basis. Facilities may follow appropriate training or exercise guidelines (e.g., National Preparedness for Response Exercise Program Guidelines) as allowed under the various regulatory requirements.

| EPA's Oil Pollution Prevention Regulation (40 CFR Part 112) | USCG-FRG (33 CFR Part 154) | DOT/RSPA-FRP (49 CFR part 194) | OSHA Emergency Action Plans (29 CFR 1910.38(a)) and Process Safety (29 CFR 1910.119) | OSHA HAZWOPER (29 CFR 1910.120) | CAA RMP (40 CFR part 68) |
|---|---|---|---|---|---|
| 112.20(h)(8) 112.21 F1.8.2 F1.8.3 | 1035(c) 1050 1055 Appendix D | 194.107(d)(1)(vii) 194.107(d)(d)(ix) 194.117 A-6 A-7 | 38(a)(5) 119(g)(1)(i) | (l)(3)(iv) (p)(8)(iii) (q)(g) | 68.95(a)(3) |

## EPA's Oil Prevention Regulation

*Self-inspection, drills/exercises, and response training.*

The response plan *shall* include:

(i) A checklist and record of inspections for tanks, secondary containment, and response equipment;

(ii) A description of the drill/exercise program to be carried out under the response plan as described in Sec. 112.21;

(iii) A description of the training program to be carried out under the response plan as described in Sec. 112.21; and

(iv) Logs of discharge prevention meetings, training sessions, and drills/exercises. These logs may be maintained as an annex to the response plan.

*Facility response training and drills/exercises.*

The owner or operator of any facility required to prepare a facility response plan under Sec. 112.20 *shall* develop and implement a facility response training program and a drill/exercise program that satisfy the requirements of this section. The owner or operator *shall* describe the programs in the response plan as provided in Sec. 112.20(h) (8).

The facility owner or operator *shall* develop a facility response training program to train those personnel involved in oil spill response activities. It is recommended that the training program be based on the USCG's Training Elements for Oil Spill Response, as applicable to facility operations. An alternative program can also be acceptable subject to approval by the Regional Administrator.

(1) The owner or operator *shall* be responsible for the proper instruction of facility personnel in the procedures to respond to discharges of oil and in applicable oil spill response laws, rules, and regulations.

(2) Training *shall* be functional in nature according to job tasks for both supervisory and non-supervisory operational personnel.

(3) Trainers *shall* develop specific lesson plans on subject areas relevant to facility personnel involved in oil spill response and cleanup.

The facility owner or operator *shall* develop a program of facility response drills/exercises, including evaluation procedures. A program that follows the National Preparedness for Response Exercise Program (PREP) (see Appendix E to this part, section 13, for availability) will be deemed satisfactory for purposes of this section. An alternative program can also be acceptable subject to approval by the Regional Administrator.

[59 FR 34101, July 1, 1994, as amended at 65 FR 40798, June 30, 2000]

**USCG-FRP**

*Training.*

A response plan submitted to meet the requirements of Secs. 154.1035 or 154.1040, as appropriate, **must** identify the training to be provided to each individual with responsibilities under the plan.

A facility owner or operator **must** identify the method to be used for training any volunteers or casual laborers used during a response to comply with the requirements of 29 CFR 1910.120.

A facility owner or operator *shall* ensure the maintenance of records sufficient to document training of facility personnel; and *shall* make them available for inspection upon request by the U.S. Coast Guard. Records for facility personnel **must** be maintained at the facility for 3 years.

Where applicable, a facility owner or operator *shall* ensure that an oil spill removal organization identified in a response plan to meet the requirements of this subpart maintains records sufficient to document training for the organization's personnel and *shall* make them available for inspection upon request by the facility's management personnel, the qualified individual, and U.S. Coast Guard. Records **must** be maintained for 3 years following completion of training.

The facility owner or operator remains responsible for ensuring that all private response personnel are trained to meet the Occupational Safety and Health Administration (OSHA) standards for emergency response operations in 29 CFR 1910.120.

*Exercises.*

A response plan submitted by an owner or operator of an MTR facility **must** include an exercise program containing both announced and unannounced exercises. The following are the minimum exercise requirements for facilities covered by this subpart:

(1) Qualified individual notification exercises (quarterly).
(2) Spill management team tabletop exercises (annually). In a 3-year period, at least one of these exercises **must** include a worst case discharge scenario.
(3) Equipment deployment exercises:
(i) Semiannually for facility owned and operated equipment.
(ii) Annually for oil spill removal organization equipment.
(4) Emergency procedures exercises (optional).
(5) Annually, at least one of the exercises listed in Sec. 154.1055(a) (2) through (4) **must** be unannounced. Unannounced means the personnel participating in the exercise **must** not be advised in advance, of the exact date, time and scenario of the exercise.
(6) The facility owner or operator *shall* design the exercise program so that all components of the response plan are exercised at least once every 3 years. All of the components do not have to be exercised at one time; they may be exercised over the 3-year period through the required exercises or through an Area exercise.

A facility owner or operator *shall* participate in unannounced exercises, as directed by the COTP. The objectives of the unannounced exercises will be to test notifications and equipment deployment for response to the average most probable discharge. After participating in an unannounced exercise directed by a COTP, the owner or operator will not be required to participate in another COTP initiated unannounced exercise for at least 3 years from the date of the exercise.

A facility owner or operator *shall* participate in Area exercises as directed by the applicable On-Scene Coordinator. The Area exercises will involve equipment deployment to respond to the spill scenario developed by the Exercise Design Team, of which the facility owner or operator will be a member. After participating in an Area exercise, a facility owner or operator will not be required to participate in another Area exercise for at least 6 years.

The facility owner or operator *shall* ensure that adequate records of all required exercises are maintained at the facility for 3 years. Records *shall* be made available to the Coast Guard upon request.

The response plan submitted to meet the requirements of this subpart **must** specify the planned exercise program. The plan **must** detail the exercise program, including the types of exercises, frequency, scope, objectives and the scheme for exercising the entire response plan every 3 years.

Compliance with the National Preparedness for Response Exercise Program (PREP) Guidelines will satisfy the facility response plan exercise requirements.

*Training Elements for Oil Spill Response Plans*

*General*

1.1 The portion of the plan dealing with training is one of the key elements of a response plan. This concept is clearly expressed by the fact that Congress, in writing OPA 90, specifically included training as one of the sections required in a vessel or facility response plan. In reviewing submitted response plans, it has been noted that the plans often do not provide sufficient information in the training section of the plan for either the user or the reviewer of the plan. In some cases, plans simply state that the crew and others will be trained in their duties and responsibilities, with no other information being provided.

In other plans, information is simply given that required parties will receive the necessary worker safety training (HAZWOPER).

1.2 The training section of the plan need not be a detailed course syllabus, but it **must** contain sufficient information to allow the user and reviewer (or evaluator) to have an understanding of those areas that are believed to be critical. Plans should identify key skill areas and the training that is required to ensure that the individual identified will be capable of performing the duties prescribed to them. It should also describe how the training will be delivered to the various personnel. Further, this section of the plan **must** work in harmony with those sections of the plan dealing with exercises, the spill management team, and the qualified individual.

1.3 The material in this appendix D is not all-inclusive and is provided for guidance only.

*Elements To Be Addressed*

2.1 To assist in the preparation of the training section of a facility response plan, some of the key elements that should be addressed are indicated in the following sections. Again, while it is not necessary that the comprehensive training program for the company be included in the response plan, it is necessary for the plan to convey the elements that define the program as appropriate.

2.2 An effective spill response training program should consider and address the following:

2.2.1 Notification requirements and procedures.

2.2.2 Communication system(s) used for the notifications.

2.2.3 Procedures to mitigate or prevent any discharge or a substantial threat of a discharge of oil resulting from failure of manifold, mechanical loading arm, or other transfer equipment or hoses, as appropriate;

2.2.3.1 Tank overfill;

2.2.3.2 Tank rupture;

2.2.3.3 Piping rupture;

2.2.3.4 Piping leak, both under pressure and not under pressure, if applicable;

2.2.3.5 Explosion or fire;

2.2.3.6 Equipment failure (e.g., pumping system failure, relief valve failure, or other general equipment relevant to operational activities associated with internal or external facility transfers).

2.2.4 Procedures for transferring responsibility for direction of response activities from facility personnel to the spill management team.

2.2.5 Familiarity with the operational capabilities of the contracted oil spill removal organizations and the procedures to notify the activate such organizations.

2.2.6 Familiarity with the contracting and ordering procedures to acquire oil spill removal organization resources.

2.2.7 Familiarity with the ACP(s).

2.2.8 Familiarity with the organizational structures that will be used to manage the response actions.

2.2.9 Responsibilities and duties of the spill management team members in accordance with designated job responsibilities.

2.2.10 Responsibilities and authority of the qualified individual as described in the facility response plan and company response organization.

2.2.11 Responsibilities of designated individuals to initiate a response and supervise response resources.

2.2.12 Actions to take, in accordance with designated job responsibilities, in the event of a transfer system leak, tank overflow, or suspected cargo tank or hull leak.

2.2.13 Information on the cargoes handled by the vessel or facility, including familiarity with—

2.2.13.1 Cargo material safety data sheets;

2.2.13.2 Chemical characteristic of the cargo;

2.2.13.3 Special handling procedures for the cargo;

2.2.13.4 Health and safety hazards associated with the cargo; and

2.2.13.5 Spill and firefighting procedures for cargo.

2.2.14 Occupational Safety and Health Administration requirements for worker health and safety (29 CFR 1910.120).

*Further Considerations*

In drafting the training section of the facility response plan, some further considerations are noted below (these points are raised simply as a reminder):

3.1 The training program should focus on training provided to facility personnel.

3.2 An organization is comprised of individuals, and a training program should be structured to recognize this fact by ensuring that training is tailored to the needs of the individuals involved in the program.

3.3 An owner or operator may identify equivalent work experience which fulfills specific training requirements.

3.4 The training program should include participation in periodic announced and unannounced exercises. This participation should approximate the actual roles and responsibilities of individual specified in the plan.

3.5 Training should be conducted periodically to reinforce the required knowledge and to ensure an adequate degree of preparedness by individuals with responsibilities under the facility response plan.

3.6 Training may be delivered via a number of different means; including classroom sessions, group discussions, video tapes, self-study workbooks, resident training courses, on-the-job training, or other means as deemed appropriate to ensure proper instruction.

3.7 New employees should complete the training program prior to being assigned job responsibilities which require participation in emergency response situations.

*Conclusion*

The information in this appendix is only intended to assist response plan preparers in reviewing the content of and in modifying the training section of their response plans. It may be more comprehensive than is needed for some facilities and not comprehensive enough for others. The Coast Guard expects that plan preparers have determined the training needs of their organizations created by the development of the response plans and the actions identified as necessary to increase the preparedness of the company and its personnel to respond to actual or threatened discharges of oil from their facilities.

## DOT/RSPA-FRP

*Training.*

Each operator *shall* conduct training to ensure that:
(1) All personnel know—
(i) Their responsibilities under the response plan,
(ii) The name and address of, and the procedure for contacting, the operator on a 24-hour basis, and
(iii) The name of, and procedures for contacting, the qualified individual on a 24-hour basis;
(2) Reporting personnel know—
(i) The content of the information summary of the response plan,
(ii) The toll-free telephone number of the National Response Center, and
(iii) The notification process; and
(3) Personnel engaged in response activities know—
(i) The characteristics and hazards of the oil discharged,

(ii) The conditions that are likely to worsen emergencies, including the consequences of facility malfunctions or failures, and the appropriate corrective actions,

(iii) The steps necessary to control any accidental discharge of oil and to minimize the potential for fire, explosion, toxicity, or environmental damage, and

(iv) The proper firefighting procedures and use of equipment, fire suits, and breathing apparatus.

(b) Each operator *shall* maintain a training record for each individual that has been trained as required by this section. These records **must** be maintained in the following manner as long as the individual is assigned duties under the response plan:

(1) Records for operator personnel **must** be maintained at the operator's headquarters; and

(2) Records for personnel engaged in response, other than operator personnel, *shall* be maintained as determined by the operator.

(c) Nothing in this section relieves an operator from the responsibility to ensure that all response personnel are trained to meet the Occupational Safety and Health Administration (OSHA) standards for emergency response operations in 29 CFR 1910.120, including volunteers or casual laborers employed during a response who are subject to those standards pursuant to 40 CFR part 311.

*Response plan: Section 6. Training Procedures*

Section 6 would include a description of the training procedures and programs of the operator.

*Response plan: Section 7. Drill Procedures*

Section 7 would include a description of the drill procedures and programs the operator uses to assess whether its response plan will function as planned. It would include:

(a) Announced and unannounced drills;

(b) The types of drills and their frequencies. For example, drills could be described as follows:

(1) Manned pipeline emergency procedures and qualified individual notification drills conducted quarterly.

(2) Drills involving emergency actions by assigned operating or maintenance personnel and notification of the qualified individual on pipeline facilities which are normally unmanned, conducted quarterly.

(3) Shore-based spill management team tabletop drills conducted yearly.

(4) Oil spill removal organization field equipment deployment drills conducted yearly.

(5) A drill that exercises the entire response plan for each response zone would be conducted at least once every 3 years.

**OSHA Process Safety**

*Training*

*Initial training.*

(i) Each employee presently involved in operating a process, and each employee before being involved in operating a newly assigned process, *shall* be trained in an overview of the process and in the operating procedures as specified in paragraph (f) of this section. The training *shall* include emphasis on the specific safety and health hazards, emergency operations including shutdown, and safe work practices applicable to the employee's job tasks.

(ii) In lieu of initial training for those employees already involved in operating a process on May 26, 1992, an employer may certify in writing that the employee has the required knowledge, skills, and abilities to safely carry out the duties and responsibilities as specified in the operating procedures.

(2) Refresher training. Refresher training *shall* be provided at least every three years, and more often if necessary, to each employee involved

in operating a process to assure that the employee understands and adheres to the current operating procedures of the process. The employer, in consultation with the employees involved in operating the process, *shall* determine the appropriate frequency of refresher training.

(3) Training documentation. The employer *shall* ascertain that each employee involved in operating a process has received and understood the training required by this paragraph. The employer *shall* prepare a record which contains the identity of the employee, the date of training, and the means used to verify that the employee understood the training.

## OSHA HAZWOPER

*Training.*

Training *shall* be based on the duties and function to be performed by each responder of an emergency response organization. The skill and knowledge levels required for all new responders, those hired after the effective date of this standard, *shall* be conveyed to them through training before they are permitted to take part in actual emergency operations on an incident. Employees who participate, or are expected to participate, in emergency response, *shall* be given training in accordance with the following paragraphs:

*First responder awareness level.*

First responders at the awareness level are individuals who are likely to witness or discover a hazardous substance release and who have been trained to initiate an emergency response sequence by notifying the proper authorities of the release. They would take no further action beyond notifying the authorities of the release. First responders at the awareness level *shall* have sufficient training or have had sufficient experience to objectively demonstrate competency in the following areas:

(A) An understanding of what hazardous substances are, and the risks associated with them in an incident.

(B) An understanding of the potential outcomes associated with an emergency created when hazardous substances are present.

(C) The ability to recognize the presence of hazardous substances in an emergency.

(D) The ability to identify the hazardous substances, if possible.

(E) An understanding of the role of the first responder awareness individual in the employer's emergency response plan including site security and control and the U.S. Department of Transportation's Emergency Response Guidebook.

(F) The ability to realize the need for additional resources, and to make appropriate notifications to the communication center.

*First responder operations level.*

First responders at the operations level are individuals who respond to releases or potential releases of hazardous substances as part of the initial response to the site for the purpose of protecting nearby persons, property, or the environment from the effects of the release. They are trained to respond in a defensive fashion without actually trying to stop the release.

Their function is to contain the release from a safe distance, keep it from spreading, and prevent exposures. First responders at the operational level *shall* have received at least eight hours of training or have had sufficient experience to objectively demonstrate competency in the following areas in addition to those listed for the awareness level and the employer *shall* so certify:

(A) Knowledge of the basic hazard and risk assessment techniques.

(B) Know how to select and use proper personal protective equipment provided to the first responder operational level.

(C) An understanding of basic hazardous materials terms.

(D) Know how to perform basic control, containment and/or confinement operations within the capabilities of the resources and personal protective equipment available with their unit.

(E) Know how to implement basic decontamination procedures.

(F) An understanding of the relevant standard operating procedures and termination procedures.

*Hazardous materials technician.*

Hazardous materials technicians are individuals who respond to releases or potential releases for the purpose of stopping the release. They assume a more aggressive role than a first responder at the operations level in that they will approach the point of release in order to plug, patch or otherwise stop the release of a hazardous substance. Hazardous materials technicians *shall* have received at least 24 hours of training equal to the first responder operations level and in addition have competency in the following areas and the employer *shall* so certify:

(A) Know how to implement the employer's emergency response plan.

(B) Know the classification, identification and verification of known and unknown materials by using field survey instruments and equipment.

(C) Be able to function within an assigned role in the Incident Command System.

(D) Know how to select and use proper specialized chemical personal protective equipment provided to the hazardous materials technician. (E) Understand hazard and risk assessment techniques.

(F) Be able to perform advance control, containment, and/or confinement operations within the capabilities of the resources and personal protective equipment available with the unit.

(G) Understand and implement decontamination procedures.

(H) Understand termination procedures.

(I) Understand basic chemical and toxicological terminology and behavior.

*Hazardous materials specialist.*

Hazardous materials specialists are individuals who respond with and provide support to hazardous materials technicians. Their duties parallel those of the hazardous materials technician, however, those duties require a more directed or specific knowledge of the various substances they may be called upon to contain. The hazardous materials specialist would also act as the site liaison with Federal, state, local and other government authorities in regards to site activities. Hazardous materials specialists *shall* have received at least 24 hours of training equal to the technician level and in addition have competency in the following areas and the employer *shall* so certify:

(A) Know how to implement the local emergency response plan.
(B) Understand classification, identification and verification of known and unknown materials by using advanced survey instruments and equipment.
(C) Know of the state emergency response plan.
(D) Be able to select and use proper specialized chemical personal protective equipment provided to the hazardous materials specialist.
(E) Understand in-depth hazard and risk techniques.
(F) Be able to perform specialized control, containment, and/or confinement operations within the capabilities of the resources and personal protective equipment available.
(G) Be able to determine and implement decontamination procedures.
(H) Have the ability to develop a site safety and control plan.
(I) Understand chemical, radiological and toxicological terminology and behavior.

*On scene incident commander.*

Incident commanders, who will assume control of the incident scene beyond the first responder awareness level, *shall* receive at least 24 hours of training equal to the first responder operations level and in addition have competency in the following areas and the employer *shall* so certify:

(A) Know and be able to implement the employer's incident command system.

(B) Know how to implement the employer's emergency response plan.

(C) Know and understand the hazards and risks associated with employees working in chemical protective clothing.

(D) Know how to implement the local emergency response plan.

(E) Know of the state emergency response plan and of the Federal Regional Response Team.

(F) Know and understand the importance of decontamination procedures.

## CAA RMP

Training for all employees in relevant procedures

# Annex 6.0: Response Critique and Plan Review and Modification Process

This annex should describe procedures for modifying the plan based on periodic plan review or lessons learned through an exercise or a response to an actual incident. Procedures to critique an actual or simulated response should be a part of this discussion. A list of plan amendments (i.e., history of updates) should also be contained in this annex. Plan modification should be viewed as a part of a facility's continuous improvement process.

| RCRA (40 CFR part 264, Subpart D, 40 CFR Part 265, Subpart D, and 40 CFR 279.52 | EPA's Oil Pollution Prevention Regulation (40 CFR Part 112) | USCG-FRG (33 CFR Part 154) | DOT/RSPA-FRP (49 CFR part 194) | OSHA Emergency Action Plans (29 CFR 1910.38(a)) and Process Safety (29 CFR 1910.119) | OSHA HAZWOPER (29 CFR 1910.120) | CAA RMP (40 CFR part 68) |
|---|---|---|---|---|---|---|
| 264.54 265.54 279.52(b)(4) | 112.20(g) | 1035(a)(6) 1035(d) 1065 D | 194.107(d)(1)(x) 194.111 194.119 194.121 A-8 | 119(l) 119(o)(1) | (l)(2)(x) (p)(8)(ii)(J) (q)(2)(x) | 68.95(a)(4) |

## RCRA

*Amendment of contingency plan.*

The contingency plan **must** be reviewed, and immediately amended, if necessary, whenever:

(a) The facility permit is revised;
(b) The plan fails in an emergency;
(c) The facility changes—in its design, construction, operation, maintenance, or other circumstances—in a way that materially increases the potential for fires, explosions, or releases of hazardous waste or hazardous waste constituents, or changes the response necessary in an emergency;y;
(d) The list of emergency coordinators changes; or
(e) The list of emergency equipment changes.

### EPA's Oil Prevention Regulation

All facility response plans *shall* be consistent with the requirements of the National Oil and Hazardous Substance Pollution Contingency Plan (40 CFR part 300) and applicable Area Contingency Plans prepared pursuant to section 311(j)(4) of the Clean Water Act. The facility response plan should be coordinated with the local emergency response plan developed by the local emergency planning committee under section 303 of Title III of the Superfund Amendments and Reauthorization Act of 1986 (42 U.S.C. 11001 et seq.). Upon request, the owner or operator should provide a copy of the facility response plan to the local emergency planning committee or State emergency response commission.

(2) The owner or operator *shall* review relevant portions of the National Oil and Hazardous Substances Pollution Contingency Plan and applicable Area Contingency Plan annually and, if necessary, revise the facility response plan to ensure consistency with these plans.

(3) The owner or operator *shall* review and update the facility response plan periodically to reflect changes at the facility.

## USCG-FRP

*Plan review and revision procedures.*

(a) A facility owner or operator **must** review his or her response plan(s) annually. This review *shall* incorporate any revisions to the plan, including listings of fish and wildlife and sensitive environments identified in the ACP in effect 6 months prior to plan review.

(1) For an MTR facility identified in Sec. 154.1015(c) of this subpart as a "significant and substantial harm facility," this review **must** occur within 1 month of the anniversary date of COTP approval of the plan. For an MTR facility identified in Sec. 154.1015(b) of this subpart, as a "substantial harm facility" this review **must** occur within 1 month of the anniversary date of submission of the plan to the COTP.

(2) The facility owner or operator *shall* submit any revision(s) to the response plan to the COTP and all other holders of the response plan for information or approval, as appropriate.

(i) Along with the revisions, the facility owner or operator *shall* submit a cover letter containing a detailed listing of all revisions to the response plan.

(ii) If no revisions are required, the facility owner or operator *shall* indicate the completion of the annual review on the record of changes page.

(iii) The COTP will review the revision(s) submitted by the owner or operator and will give written notice to the owner or operator of any COTP objection(s) to the proposed revisions within 30 days of the date the revision(s) were submitted to the COTP. The revisions *shall* become effective not later than 30 days from their submission to the COTP unless the COTP indicates otherwise in writing as provided in this paragraph. If the COTP indicates that the revision(s) need to be modified before implementation, the owner or operator will modify the revision(s) within the time period set by the COTP.

(3) Any required revisions **must** be entered in the plan and noted on the record of changes page.

(b) The facility owner or operator *shall* submit revisions to a previously submitted or approved plan to the COTP and all other holders of the response plan for information or approval within 30 days, whenever there is—

(1) A change in the facility's configuration that significantly affects the information included in the response plan;

(2) A change in the type of oil (petroleum oil group) handled, stored, or transported that affects the required response resources;

(3) A change in the name(s) or capabilities of the oil spill removal organization required by Sec. 154.1045;

(4) A change in the facility's emergency response procedures;

(5) A change in the facility's operating area that includes ports or geographic area(s) not covered by the previously approved plan. A facility may not operate in an area not covered in a plan previously submitted or approved, as appropriate, unless the revised plan is approved or interim operating approval is received under Sec. 154.1025; or

(6) Any other changes that significantly affect the implementation of the plan.

(c) Except as required in paragraph (b) of this section, revisions to personnel and telephone number lists included in the response plan do not require COTP approval. The COTP and all other holders of the response plan *shall* be advised of these revisions and provided a copy of the revisions as they occur.

(d) The COTP may require a facility owner or operator to revise a response plan at any time as a result of a compliance inspection if the COTP determines that the response plan does not meet the requirements of this subpart or as a result of inadequacies noted in the response plan during an actual pollution incident at the facility.

## DOT/RSPA-FRP

*Response plan retention.*

(a) Each operator *shall* maintain relevant portions of its response plan at the following locations:
(1) The response plan at the operator's headquarters;
(2) The core plan and relevant response zone appendices for each line section whose pressure may be affected by the operation of a particular pump station, at that pump station; and
(3) The core plan and relevant response zone appendices at any other locations where response activities may be conducted.
(b) Each operator *shall* provide a copy of its response plan to each qualified individual.

*Submission and approval procedures.*

(a) Each operator *shall* submit two copies of the response plan required by this part. Copies of the response plan *shall* be submitted to: Pipeline Response Plans Officer, Research and Special Programs Administration, Department of Transportation, 400 Seventh Street, SW., Washington, DC 20590-0001.
(b) If RSPA determines that a response plan requiring approval does not meet all the requirements of this part, RSPA will notify the operator of any alleged deficiencies, and to provide the operator an opportunity to respond, including the opportunity for an informal conference, on any proposed plan revisions and an opportunity to correct any deficiencies.
(c) An operator who disagrees with the RSPA determination that a plan contains alleged deficiencies may petition RSPA for reconsideration within 30 days from the date of receipt of RSPA's notice. After considering all relevant material presented in writing or at an informal conference, RSPA will notify the operator of its final decision. The operator **must** comply with the final decision within 30 days of issuance unless RSPA allows additional time.

(d) For those response zones of pipelines, described in Sec. 194.103(c), that could reasonably be expected to cause significant and substantial harm, RSPA will approve the response plan if RSPA determines that the response plan meets all requirements of this part, and the OSC raises no objection.

(e) If RSPA has not approved a response plan for a pipeline described in Sec. 194.103(c), the operator may submit a certification to RSPA by July 18, 1993, that the operator has obtained, through contract or other approved means, the necessary private personnel and equipment to respond, to the maximum extent practicable, to a worst case discharge or a substantial threat of such a discharge. The certificate **must** be signed by the qualified individual or an appropriate corporate officer.

(f) If RSPA receives a request from an OSC to review a response plan, RSPA may require an operator to provide a copy of the response plan to the OSC. If an OSC recommends that an operator not previously required to submit a plan to RSPA, should submit one, RSPA will require the operator to prepare and submit a response plan and send a copy to the OSC.

*Response plan review and update procedures.*

(a) Each operator *shall* review its response plan at least every 5 years from the date of submission and modify the plan to address new or different operating conditions or information included in the plan.

(b) If a new or different operating condition or information would substantially affect the implementation of a response plan, the operator **must** immediately modify its response plan to address such a change and, within 30 days of making such a change, submit the change to RSPA. Examples of changes in operating conditions that would cause a significant change to an operator's response plan are:

(1) An extension of the existing pipeline or construction of a new pipeline in a response zone not covered by the previously approved plan;

(2) Relocation or replacement of the pipeline in a way that substantially affects the information included in the response plan, such as a change to the worst case discharge volume;

(3) The type of oil transported, if the type affects the required response resources, such as a change from crude oil to gasoline;

(4) The name of the oil spill removal organization;

(5) Emergency response procedures;

(6) The qualified individual;

(7) A change in the NCP or an ACP that has significant impact on the equipment appropriate for response activities; and

(8) Any other information relating to circumstances that may affect full implementation of the plan.

(c) If RSPA determines that a change to a response plan does not meet the requirements of this part, RSPA will notify the operator of any alleged deficiencies, and provide the operator an opportunity to respond, including an opportunity for an informal conference, to any proposed plan revisions and an opportunity to correct any deficiencies.

(d) An operator who disagrees with a determination that proposed revisions to a plan are deficient may petition RSPA for reconsideration, within 30 days from the date of receipt of RSPA's notice. After considering all relevant material presented in writing or at the conference, RSPA will notify the operator of its final decision. The operator **must** comply with the final decision within 30 days of issuance unless RSPA allows additional time.

*Response plan: Section 8. Response Plan Review and Update Procedures*

Section 8 would include the following:

(a) Procedures to meet Sec. 194.121; and

(b) Procedures to review the plan after a worst case discharge and to evaluate and record the plan's effectiveness.

## OSHA Process Safety

*Management of change.*

(1) The employer *shall* establish and implement written procedures to manage changes (except for "replacements in kind") to process chemicals, technology, equipment, and procedures; and, changes to facilities that affect a covered process.

(2) The procedures *shall* assure that the following considerations are addressed prior to any change:

(i) The technical basis for the proposed change;

(ii) Impact of change on safety and health;

(iii) Modifications to operating procedures;

(iv) Necessary time period for the change; and,

(v) Authorization requirements for the proposed change.

(3) Employees involved in operating a process and maintenance and contract employees whose job tasks will be affected by a change in the process *shall* be informed of, and trained in, the change prior to start-up of the process or affected part of the process.

(4) If a change covered by this paragraph results in a change in the process safety information required by paragraph (d) of this section, such information *shall* be updated accordingly.

(5) If a change covered by this paragraph results in a change in the operating procedures or practices required by paragraph (f) of this section, such procedures or practices *shall* be updated accordingly.

o) Compliance Audits. (1) Employers *shall* certify that they have evaluated compliance with the provisions of this section at least every three years to verify that the procedures and practices developed under the standard are adequate and are being followed.

(2) The compliance audit *shall* be conducted by at least one person knowledgeable in the process.

(3) A report of the findings of the audit *shall* be developed.

(4) The employer *shall* promptly determine and document an appropriate response to each of the findings of the compliance audit, and document that deficiencies have been corrected.

(5) Employers *shall* retain the two (2) most recent compliance audit reports.

**OSHA HAZWOPER**

Critique of response and follow-up

**CAA RMP**

Procedures to review and update, as appropriate, the emergency response plan to reflect changes at the stationary source and ensure that employees are informed of changes

# Annex 7.0: Prevention

Some federal regulations that primarily address prevention of accidents include elements that relate to contingency planning (e.g., EPA's RMP and SPCC regulations and OSHA's Process Safety Standard).

This annex is designed to allow facilities to include prevention-based requirements (e.g., maintenance, testing, in-house inspections, release detection, site security, containment, fail safe engineering) that are required in contingency planning regulations or that have the potential to impact response activities covered in a contingency plan. The modular nature of the suggested plan outline provides planners with necessary flexibility to include prevention requirements in the ICP. This annex may not need to be submitted to regulatory agencies for review.

| OSHA HAZWOPER (29 CFR 1910.120) |
|---|
| (l)(2)(iii) |
| (p)(8)(ii)(C) |
| (q)(2)(iii) |

## OSHA HAZWOPER

On a daily basis, individual personnel should be constantly alert for indicators of potentially hazardous situations and for signs and symptoms in themselves and others that warn of hazardous conditions and exposures. Rapid recognition of dangerous situations can avert an emergency and prevent injuries and loss of life. Regular health and safety meetings with employees should address:

- Tasks to be performed;
- Time constraints (e.g., rest breaks, air tank changes);
- Hazards that may be encountered, including their potential effects, how to recognize symptoms or monitor them, concentration limits, or other danger signals; and
- Emergency procedures.

After daily work assignments, a debriefing session should be held to review work accomplished, problems observed, and suggestions for future improvement.

# Annex 8: Regulatory Compliance and Cross-Reference Matrices

This annex should include information necessary for plan reviewers to determine compliance with specific regulatory requirements. To the extent that plan drafters did not include regulatory required elements in the balance of the ICP, they should be addressed in this annex. This annex should also include signatory pages to convey management approval and certifications required by the regulations, such as certification of adequate response resources and/or statements of regulatory applicability as required by regulations under OPA authority. Finally, this annex should contain cross-references that indicate where specific regulatory requirements are addressed in the ICP for each regulation covered under the plan.

Federal Register / Vol. 61, No. 109 / Wednesday, June 5, 1996 / Notices     28657

## ATTACHMENT 3: REGULATORY CROSS-COMPARISON MATRICES

| RCRA (40 CFR Part 264 Subpart D[1], 40 CFR Part 265 Subpart D[2], 40 CFR Part 279.52(b)[3]) | ICP Citation(s) |
|---|---|
| 264.52 Content of contingency plan: | |
| (a) Emergency response actions.[4] | |
| (b) Amendments to SPCC plan | |
| (c) Coordination with State and local response parties[5] | II.2.b; III.3.a. |
| (d) Emergency coordinator(s) | II.2.a; III.2. |
| (e) Detailed description of emergency equipment on-site | II.2.d.(3); II.2.e; II.2.f; III.3.f.(1); III.3.f.(3); III.3.f.(4). |
| (f) Evacuation plan if applicable | III.3.b.(3). |
| 264.53 Copies of contingency plan. | |
| 264.54 Amendment of contingency plan | III.6. |
| 264.55 Emergency coordinator | II.2.a; III.3.b.(1). |
| 264.56 Emergency procedures: | |
| (a) Notification | II.2.a; III.2; III.3.b.(2). |
| (b) Emergency identification/characterization | II.2.c; III.3.c.(3). |
| (c) Health/environmental assessment | II.2.c; III.3.c.(3). |
| (d) Reporting | II.2.a; III.2; III.3.c.(3). |
| (e) Containment | III.3.c.(2); III.3.c.(4). |
| (f) Monitoring | III.3.b.(3); III.3.c.(3). |
| (g) Treatment, storage, or disposal of wastes | III.3.d.(4). |
| (h) Cleanup procedures: | |
| (1) Disposal | III.3.d.(4). |
| (2) Decontamination | III.3.c.(6). |
| (i) Follow-up procedures | II.4. |
| (j) Follow-up report | III.4.a. |
| 265.52 Content of contingency plan: | |
| (a) Emergency response actions.[4] | |
| (b) Amendments to SPCC plan | |
| (c) Coordination with State and local response parties[7] | II.2.b; III.3.a. |
| (d) Emergency coordinator(s) | II.2.a; III.2. |
| (e) Detailed description of emergency equipment on-site | II.2.d.(3); II.2.e; II.2.f; III.3.f.(1); III.3.f.(3); III.3.f.(4). |
| (f) Evacuation plan if applicable | III.3.b.(3). |
| 265.53 Copies of contingency plan. | |
| 265.54 Amendment of contingency plan | III.6. |
| 265.55 Emergency coordinator | II.2.a; III.3.b.(1). |
| 265.56 Emergency procedures: | |
| (a) Notification | II.2.a; III.2; III.3.b.(2). |
| (b) Emergency identification/characterization | II.2.c; III.3.c.(3). |
| (c) Health/environmental assessment | II.2.c; III.3.c.(3). |
| (d) Reporting | II.2.a; III.2; III.3.c.(3). |
| (e) Containment | III.3.c.(2); III.3.c.(4). |
| (f) Monitoring | III.3.b.(3); III.3.c.(3). |
| (g) Treatment, storage, or disposal of wastes | III.3.d.(4). |
| (h) Cleanup procedures: | |
| (1) Disposal | III.3.d.(4). |
| (2) Decontamination | III.3.c.(6). |
| (i) Follow-up procedures | II.4. |
| (j) Follow-up report | III.4.a. |
| 279.52(b)(2) Content of contingency plan: | |
| (i) Emergency response actions[4] | |
| (ii) Amendments to SPCC plan. | |
| (iii) Coordination with State and local response parties[6] | II.2.b; III.3.a. |
| (iv) Emergency coordinator(s) | II.2.a; III.2. |
| (v) Detailed description of emergency equipment on-site | II.2.d.(3); II.2.e; II.2.f; III.3.f.(1); III.3.f.(3); III.3.f.(4). |
| (vi) Evacuation plan if applicable | III.3.b.(3). |
| (3) Copies of contingency plan. | |
| (4) Amendment of contingency plan | III.6. |
| (5) Emergency coordinator | II.2.a; III.3.b.(1). |
| (6) Emergency procedures: | |
| (i) Notification | II.2.a; III.2; III.3.b.(2). |
| (ii) Emergency identification/characterization | II.2.c; III.3.c.(3). |
| (iii) Health/environmental assessment | II.2.c; III.3.c.(3). |
| (iv) Reporting | II.2.a; III.2; III.3.c.(3). |
| (v) Containment | III.3.c.(2); III.3.c.(4). |
| (vi) Monitoring | III.3.b.(3); III.3.c.(3). |
| (vii) Treatment, storage, or disposal of wastes | III.3.d.(4). |
| (viii) Cleanup procedures: | |
| (A) Disposal | III.3.d.(4). |
| (B) Decontamination | III.3.c.(6). |

## ATTACHMENT 3: REGULATORY CROSS-COMPARISON MATRICES—Continued

| | ICP Citation(s) |
|---|---|
| (ix) Follow-up report ............................................................................... | III.4.a. |

| EPA's Oil Pollution Prevention Regulation (40 CFR 112) | |
|---|---|
| 112.7(d)(1)  Strong spill contingency plan and written commitment of manpower, equipment, and materials.¹⁴,¹⁵ | |
| 112.20(g)  General response planning requirements ..................................... | III.3.d.(3); III.6. |
| 112.20(h)  Response plan elements ............................................................... | I.2; III.8. |
| (1) Emergency response action plan (Appendix F1.1); | |
| (i) Identify and telephone number of qualified individual (F1.2.6) ........ | III.3.b.(1). |
| (ii) Identity of individuals/organizations to contact if there is a discharge (F1.3.1) ......... | III.2. |
| (iii) Description of information to pass to response personnel in event of a reportable spill (F1.3). | II.2.a. |
| (iv) Description of facility's response equipment and its location (F1.3.2) ............... | II.2.d.(3);  III.3.e.(3);  III.3.e.(6);  III.3.f.(1); III.3.f.(3). |
| (v) Description of response personnel capabilities (F1.3.4) ................ | II.2.b; III.3; III.3.e.(5); III.3.f.(2); |
| (vi) Plans for evacuation of the facility and a reference to community evacuation plans (F1.3.5). | III.3.b.(3); III.3.e.(5) |
| (vii) Description of immediate measures to secure the source (F1.7.1) ........ | II.2.d.(2); III.3.c.(2); III.3.c.(4). |
| (viii) Diagram of the facility (F1.9) ............................................... | III.1.a–b. |
| (2) Facility information (F1.2, F2.0) ................................................. | I.4.b–d; III.1. |
| (3) Information about emergency responses: | |
| (i) Identify of private personnel and equipment to remove to the maximum extent practicable a WCD or other discharges (F1.3.2, F1.3.4). | III.3.c.(2);  III.3.c.(4)–(5);  III.3.e.(6). |
| (ii) Evidence of contracts or other approved means for ensuring personnel and equipment availability. | III.3.e.(5); III.3.f.(5) |
| (iii) Identity and telephone of individuals/organizations to be contacted in event of a discharge (F1.3.1). | II.2.a; III.2.b–d; III.3.b.(2). |
| (iv) Description of information to pass to response personnel in event of a reportable spill (F1.3.1). | II.2.a. |
| (v) Description of response personnel capabilities (F1.3.4) ................ | II.2.b; III.3; III.3.e.(5); III.3.f.(2). |
| (vi) Description of a facility's response equipment, location of the equipment, and equipment testing (F1.3.2, F1.3.3). | II.2.d.(3);  III.3.e.(3);  III.3.e.(6);  III.3.f.(1); III.3.f.(3). |
| (vii) Plans for evacuation of the facility and a reference to community evacuation plans as appropriate (F1.3.5). | III.3.b.(3); III.3.e.(5). |
| (viii) Diagram of evacuation routes (F1.9). ..................................... | III.3.b.(3). |
| (ix) Duties of the qualified individual (F1.3.6) ................................. | II.2c;  II.2.d.(1);  I.2.e;  III.2.b–c;  III.3.c.(3); III.3.d.(1); III.3.f. |
| (4) Hazard evaluation (F1.4) ........................................................ | II.2c; III.3.d.(1); III.4.b. |
| (5) Response planning levels (F1.5, F1.5.1, F15.2) .......................... | III.3.d.(1). |
| (6) Discharge detection systems (F1.6, F1.6.1, F1.6.2) ................... | II.1. |
| (7) Plan implementation (F1.7) ...................................................... | II.2.d–f; II.3; III.4. |
| (i) Response actions to be carried out (F1.7.1.1) ...................... | II.2; III.3.d.(2). |
| (ii) Description of response equipment to be used for each scenario (F1.7.1.1) ........ | III.3.d.(1). |
| (iii) Plans to dispose of contaminated cleanup materials (F1.7.3) ... | III.3.c.(5)–(6) |
| (iv) Measures to provide adequate containment and drainage of spilled oil (F1.7.3) ... | III.3.c.(2); III.3.c.(4); III.3.d.(2); III.3.d.(4). |
| (8) Self-inspection, drills/exercises, and response training (F1.8.1–F1.8.3.2) .......... | III.3.e.(6); III.5. |
| (9) Diagrams (F1.9) ...................................................................... | III.1.b. |
| (10) Security systems (F1.10) ....................................................... | III.3.e.(2). |
| (11) Response plan cover sheet (F2.0). | |
| 112.21  Facility response training and drills/exercises (F1.8.2, F1.8.3) ............... | III.5. |
| Appendix F Facility-Specific Response Plan: ¹² | I.2. |
| 1.0  Model Facility-Specific Response Plan. | |
| 1.1  Emergency Response Action Plan. | |
| 1.2  Facility Information ........................................................... | I.3; I.4.a; I.4.b–c; I.4.h; II.2.a; III.1. |
| 1.3  Emergency Response Information: | |
| 1.3.1  Notification ............................................................... | II.2a; III.2a–c. |
| 1.3.2  Response Equipment List ......................................... | II.2.d.(3); III.3.e.(3); III.3.f.(1); III.3.f.(3)–(4). |
| 1.3.3  Response Equipment Testing/Deployment ................ | III.3.e.(6). |
| 1.3.4  Personnel ................................................................ | II.2.b; III.3; III.3.f.(2). |
| 1.3.5  Evacuation Plans ..................................................... | III.3.b.(3); III.3.e.(5) |
| 1.3.6  Qualified Individual's Duties .................................... | II.2. |
| 1.4  Hazard Evaluation ........................................................ | II.2.c. |
| 1.4.1  Hazard Identification ................................................ | III.1.c; III.3.d.(1). |
| 1.4.2  Vulnerability Analysis .............................................. | II.2c; III.3.d.(1). |
| 1.4.3  Analysis of the Potential for an Oil Spill .................... | III.3.d.(1). |
| 1.4.4  Facility Reportable Oil Spill History .......................... | III.4.b. |
| 1.5  Discharge Scenarios: | |
| 1.5.1  Small and Medium Discharges ................................. | III.3.d.(1). |
| 1.5.2  Worst Case Discharge ............................................ | III.3.d.(1). |
| 1.6  Discharge Detection Systems: | |
| 1.6.1  Discharge Detection By Personnel ........................... | II.1. |

Federal Register / Vol. 61, No. 109 / Wednesday, June 5, 1996 / Notices     28659

## ATTACHMENT 3: REGULATORY CROSS-COMPARISON MATRICES—Continued

| | ICP Citation(s) |
|---|---|
| 1.6.2   Automated Discharge Detection ........................................................ | II.1. |
| 1.7   Plan Implementation ............................................................................. | II.2. |
|    1.7.1   Response Resources for Small, Medium, and Worst Case Spills ......... | II.2.d.(3); II.2.f; III.3.c.(3); III.3.d.(2); III.3.f.(1); III.3.f.(3)–(4). |
|    1.7.2   Disposal Plans ............................................................................ | III.3.c.(5)–(6); III.3.d.(4). |
|    1.7.3   Containment and Drainage Planning ........................................ | II.2.d; III.3.c.(4); III.3.d.(2). |
| 1.8   Self-inspection, Drills/Exercises, and Response Training: | |
|    1.8.1   Facility Self-inspection ................................................................ | III.3.e.(6). |
|    1.8.2   Facility Drills.Exercises ............................................................. | III.5. |
|    1.8.3   Response Training ....................................................................... | III.5. |
| 1.9   Diagrams ............................................................................................... | I.4; III.1.a–c. |
| 1.10   Security ................................................................................................ | III.3.e.(2). |
| 2.0   Response Plan Cover Sheet ................................................................ | I.4.b; I.4.c; I.4.h; III.1. |
| **USCG FRP (33 CFR part 154)** | |
| 154.1026   Qualified individual and alternate qualified individual ................ | II.2.a; III.3.b.(1). |
| 154.1028   Availability of response resources by contract or other approved means ... | III.3.f.cr III.8; III.3.f.(5). |
| 154.1029   Worst case discharge ............................................................... | III.3.d.(1). |
| 154.1030   General response plan contents:. | |
|   (a) The plan must be written in English. | |
|   (b) Organization of the plan [13] ...................................................... | I.2. |
|   (c) Required contents. | |
|   (d) Sactions submitted to COTP. | |
|   (e) Cross-references ........................................................................ | III.8. |
|   (f) Consistency with NCP and ACPs ............................................. | III.3.d.(3). |
| 154.1035   Significant and substantial harm facilities: | |
|   (a) Introduction and plan content ..................................................... | III.1. |
|    (1) Facility's name, physical and mailing address, county, telephone, and fax ...... | I.4.a; I.4.c–d; I.4.h–l |
|    (2) Description of a facility's location in a manner that could aid in locating the facility | I.4.c. |
|    (3) Name, address, and procedures for contacting the owner/operator on 24-hour basis. | I.4.b; II.2.a |
|    (4) Table of contents .................................................................... | I.2. |
|    (5) Cross index, if appropriate ...................................................... | III.8. |
|    (6) Record of change(s) to record information on plan updates ...... | I.3; III.8. |
|   (b) Emergency Response Action Plan: | |
|    (1) Notification procedures: | |
|     (i) Prioritized list identifying person(s), including name, telephone number, and role in plan, to be notified in event of threat or actual discharge. | II.2.a; III.2.a–c. |
|     (ii) Information to be provided in initial and follow-up notifications to federal, state, and local agencies. | III.3.b; II.2.a–c. |
|    (2) Facility's spill mitigation procedures [14] ............................... | II.2.d.(2); III.3.c.(2). |
|     (i) Volume(s) of persistent and non-persistent oil groups. | II.2. |
|     (ii) Prioritized procedures/task delegation to mitigate or prevent a potential or actual discharge or emergencies involving certain equipment/scenarios. | II.2. |
|     (iii) List of equipment and responsibilities of facility personnel to mitigate an average most probable discharge. | II.2.e–f; III.3.f.(3); III.3.c.(1)–(5). |
|    (3) Facility response activities [15] ............................................. | II.2.c; II.2.e–f; II.3; II.4; III.3.c.(3). |
|     (i) Description of facility personnel's responsibilities to initiate/supervise response until arrival of qualified individual. | II.1; II.2. |
|     (ii) Qualified individual's responsibilities/authority ................... | II.2. |
|     (iii) Facility or corporate organizational structure used to manage response actions | II.2.b; II.3; III.3.a; III.3.b.(2)–(4); III.3.c; III.3.d.(1); III.3.e–f. |
|     (iv) Oil spill response organization(s)/spill management team available by contract or other approved means. | II.2.d.(3); III.3.c.(4)–(5); III.3.e.(6); III.3.f.(1)–(2); III.3.f.(5). |
|     (v) For mobile facilities that operate in more than one COTP, the oil spill response organization(s)/spill management team in the applicable geographic-specific appendix. | II.2.d.(3). |
|    (4) Fish and wildlife sensitive environments ............................... | III.1.c; III.3.d.(1)–(2). |
|     (i) Areas of economic importance and environmental sensitivity as identified in the ACP that are potentially impacted by a WCD. | II.2.c. |
|     (ii) List areas and provide maps/charts and describe response actions. | |
|     (iii) Equipment and personnel necessary to protect identified areas ...... | II.2.e–f; III.3.f.(3); III.3.c.(1)–(5). |
|    (5) Disposal plan ............................................................................ | III.3.d.(4). |
|   (c) Training and exercises .................................................................. | III.5. |
|   (d) Plan review and update procedures ............................................. | III.6. |
|   (e) Appendices .................................................................................... | I.4.c; III.1.b. |
|    (1) Facility specific information ...................................................... | III.1. |
|    (2) List of contacts ........................................................................ | II.2.a; III.2.a–c; III.3.b.(1). |
|    (3) Equipment lists and records .................................................... | III.3.e.(3); III.3.e.(6); III.3.f.(1); III.3.f.(3)–(5). |
|    (4) Communications plan ............................................................... | III.3.b.(2). |
|    (5) Site-specific safety and health plan ........................................ | III.3.b.(3); III.3.c.(7); III.3.e. (1). |

28660    Federal Register / Vol. 61, No. 109 / Wednesday, June 5, 1996 / Notices

## ATTACHMENT 3: REGULATORY CROSS-COMPARISON MATRICES—Continued

| | ICP Citation(s) |
|---|---|
| (6) List of acronyms and definitions. | |
| (7) A geographic-specific appendix. | |
| 154.1040  Specific requirements for substantial harm facilities. | |
| 154.1041  Specific response information to be maintained on mobile MTR facilities. | |
| 154.1045  Groups I–IV petroleum oils. | |
| 154.1047  Group V petroleum oils. | |
| 154.1050  Training | III.5. |
| 154.1055  Drills | III.5. |
| 154.1057  Inspection and maintenance of response resources | III.3.e.(6). |
| 154.1060  Submission and approval procedures. | |
| 154.1065  Plan revision and amendment procedures | III.6. |
| 154.1070  Deficiencies. | |
| 154.1075  Appeal Process. | |
| Appendix C—Guidelines for determining and evaluating required response resources for facility response plans. | III.3.f.(3). |
| Appendix D—Training elements for oil spill response plans | III.5. |
| **DOT/RSPA FRP (49 CFR Part 194)** | |
| 194.101  Operators required to submit plans. | |
| 194.103  Significant and substantial harm: operator's statement | III.8. |
| 194.105  Worst case discharge | III.3.d.(1). |
| 194.107  General response plan requirements: | |
| (a) Resource planning requirements | III.3.d. |
| (b) Language requirements. | |
| (c) Consistency with NCP and ACP(s) | III.3.d.(3); III.8. |
| (d) Each response plan must include: | |
| (1) Core Plan Contents: | |
| i) An information summary as required in 194.113 | I.4; III.1. |
| 194.113(a)  Core plan information summary: | |
| (1) Name and address of operator | I.4.b; I.4.d. |
| (2) Description of each response zone | I.4.c. |
| (b) Response zone appendix information summary: | |
| (1) Core plan information summary | I.4; III.1. |
| (2) Name^O^S^A^A^O Submission and approval procedures | III.6. |
| 194.121  Response plan review and update procedures | III.6. |
| ^Apendix^S^A^Recommended guidelines for the preparation of response plans | I.2. |
| Section 1—Information summary | I.4.b–c; II.2.a; II.2.f.; III.8. |
| Section 2—Notification procedures | II.2.a; III.2; III.3.b.(2); III.3.e.(3). |
| Section 3—Spill detection and on-scene spill mitigation procedures | II.1; II.2.e–f; III.3.c.(2). |
| Section 4—Response activities | II.2.b; III.3.b.(1). |
| Section 5—List of contacts | II.2.a. |
| Section 6—Training procedures | III.5. |
| Section 7—Drill procedures | III.5. |
| Section 8—Response plan review and update procedures | III.6. |
| Section 9—Response zone appendices | II.2.b; II.3; III.1.a–c; III.3. |
| **OSHA Emergency Action Plans (29 CFR 1910.38(a)) and Process Safety (29 CFR 1910.119)** | |
| 1910.38(a)  Emergency action plan: | |
| (1) Scope and applicability | III.3.c.(1); III.3.d. |
| (2) Elements: | |
| (i) Emergency escape procedures and emergency escape route assignments | II.2; II.2.c; III.3.b.(3); III.3.c. |
| (ii) Procedures to be followed by employees who remain to operate critical plant operations before they evacuate. | II.2; II.2.c; II.2.e; III.3.c. |
| (iii) Procedures to account for all employees after emergency evacuation has been completed. | II.2.a; III.3.b.(2); III.3.b.(3); III.3.c; III.4. |
| (iv) Rescue and medical duties for those employees who are to perform them | III.3.b.(3); III.3.c; III.3.e.(7); III.3.e.(1). |
| (v) The preferred means of reporting fires and other emergencies | II.2.a; III.3.b. |
| (vi) Names or regular job titles of persons or departments who can be contacted for further information or explanation of duties under the plan. | I.4.f; II.2.a; III.3.b.(2); III.3.b.(4). |
| (3) Alarm system ** | II.2.a; III.3.c.(3); III.3.e.(3). |
| (4) Evacuation | II.2.d; III.3.b.(3); III.3.c.(3); III.3.d; III.3.d.(1). |
| (5) Training | III.3.e.(5); III.5. |
| 1910.119  Process safety management of highly hazardous chemicals: | |
| (e)(3)(ii)  Investigation of previous incidents | III.4; III.4.b. |
| (e)(3)(ii)  Process hazard analysis requirements | III.3.e.(3). |
| (g)(1)(i)  Employee training in process/operating procedures | III.5. |
| (j)(4)  Inspection/testing of process equipment | III.3.e.(6). |
| (j)(5)  Equipment repair | III.3.e.(6). |
| (l)  Management of change(s) | III.5. |
| (m)  Incident investigation | III.4.a. |

Federal Register / Vol. 61, No. 109 / Wednesday, June 5, 1996 / Notices 28661

ATTACHMENT 3: REGULATORY CROSS-COMPARISON MATRICES—Continued

| | ICP Citation(s) |
|---|---|
| (n) Emergency planning and response | I.1; II.1; II.2; II.2.d; III.2; III.2.a; III.2.b. |
| (o)(1) Certification of compliance | III.6. |
| 1910.165 Employee alarm systems: | |
| (b) General requirements | III.3.e.(3). |
| (b)(1) Purpose of alarm system | III.2; III.2.a. |
| (b)(4) Preferred means of reporting emergencies | III.2. |
| (d) Maintenance and testing | III.3.e.(6). |
| 1910.272 Grain handling facilities: | |
| (d) Development/implementation of emergency action plan | I.1; III.2. |

OSHA HAZWOPER (29 CFR 1910.120)

| | |
|---|---|
| 1910.120(k) Decontamination | III.3.c.(6). |
| 1910.120(l) Emergency response program | I.1. |
| (1) Emergency response plan: | |
| (i) An emergency response plan shall be developed and implemented by all employers within the scope of this section to handle anticipated emergencies prior to the commencement of hazardous waste operations. | |
| (ii) Employers who will evacuate their employees from the workplace when an emergency occurs, and who do not permit any of their employees to assist in handling the emergency, are exempt from the requirements of this paragraph if they provide an emergency action plan complying with section 1910.38(a) of this part. | |
| (2) Elements of an emergency response plan: | |
| (i) Pre-emergency planning and coordination with outside parties | I.4.f; II.2.b; II.2.c; III.2.b; III.2.c; III.3.b.(4); III.3.d. |
| (ii) Personnel roles, lines of authority, and communication | I.4.f; II.2.b; III.2.a; III.2.c; III.3.b.(4); III.3.e.(4). |
| (iii) Emergency recognition and prevention | II.1; III.7. |
| (iv) Safe distances and places of refuge | III.3.b.(3); III.3.d.(2). |
| (v) Site security and control | III.3.d.(2); III.3.e.(2) |
| (vi) Evacuation routes and procedures | II.2.d; III.3.b.(3) |
| (vii) Decontamination procedures | III.3.c.(6). |
| (viii) Emergency medical treatment and response procedures | II.2.d; III.3.c.(7); III.3.e.(1). |
| (ix) Emergency alerting and response procedures | II.2; II.2.a; II.2.f; II.4; III.2; III.2.a; III.2.b; III.2.c; III.3.d. |
| (x) Critique of response and follow-up | II.3; III.4; III.4.a; III.6. |
| (xi) PPE and emergency equipment | III.3.e.(6); III.3.f.(3); III.3.d.(2); III.3.e.(6); III.3.f.(3). |
| (3) Procedures for handling emergency incidents: | |
| (i) Additional elements of emergency response plans: | |
| (A) Site topography, layout, and prevailing weather conditions | III.1.c. |
| (B) Procedures for reporting incidents to local, state, and federal government agencies. | II.2.a; III.2. |
| (ii) The emergency response plan shall be a separate section of the Site Safety and Health Plan. | |
| (iii) The emergency response plan shall be compatible with the disaster, fire, and/or emergency response plans of local, state, and federal agencies. | III.3.e. |
| (iv) The emergency response plan shall be rehearsed regularly as part of the overall training program for site operations. | III.6. |
| (v) The site emergency response plan shall be reviewed periodically and, as necessary, be amended to keep it current with new or changing site conditions or information. | |
| (vi) An employee alarm system shall be installed in accordance with 29 CFR 1910.165 to notify employees of an emergency situation; to stop work activities if necessary; to lower background noise in order to speed communications; and to begin emergency procedures. | |
| (vii) Based upon the information available at time of the emergency, the employer shall evaluate the incident and the site response capabilities and proceed with the appropriate steps to implement the site emergency response plan. | II.2.c; II.2.d. |
| 1910.120(p)(8) Emergency response program: | I.1 |
| (i) Emergency response plan. | |
| (ii) Elements of an emergency response plan: | |
| (A) Pre-emergency planning and coordination with outside parties | I.4.f; II.2.b; II.2.c; III.2.b; III.2.c; III.3.b.(4); III.3.d. |
| (B) Personnel roles, lines of authority, and communication | I.4.f; II.2.b; III.2.c; III.2.c; III.3.b.(4); III.3.e.(4). |
| (C) Emergency recognition and prevention | II.1; III.7 |
| (D) Safe distances and places of refuge | III.3.b.(3); III.3.d.(2) |
| (E) Site security and control | III.3.d.(2); III.3.e.(2) |
| (F) Evacuation routes and procedures | II.2.d; III.3.b.(3). |
| (G) Decontamination procedures | III.3.c.(6). |
| (H) Emergency medical treatment and response procedures | II.2.d; III.3.c.(7); III.3.e.(1). |
| (I) Emergency alerting and response procedures | II.2; II.2.a; II.2.f; II.4; III.2; III.2.a; III.2.b; III.2.c; III.3.d. |

28662     Federal Register / Vol. 61, No. 109 / Wednesday, June 5, 1996 / Notices

ATTACHMENT 3: REGULATORY CROSS-COMPARISON MATRICES—Continued

| | ICP Citation(s) |
|---|---|
| (J) Critique of response and follow-up | II.3; III.4; III.4.a; III.6. |
| (K) PPE and emergency equipment | III.3.e.(6); III.3.f.(3); III.3.d.(2); III.3.e.(6); III.3.f.(3). |
| (iii) Training | III.6. |
| (iv) Procedures for handling emergency incidents: | |
| (A) Additional elements of emergency response plans: | |
| (1) Site topography, layout, and prevailing weather conditions | III.1.c; III.3.d.(1). |
| (2) Procedures for reporting incidents to local, state, and federal government agencies. | II.2.a; III.2. |
| (B) The emergency response plan shall be compatible and integrated with the disaster, fire and/or emergency response plans of local, state, and federal agencies. | III.3.e. |
| (C) The emergency response plan shall be rehearsed regularly as part of the overall training program for site operations. | |
| (D) The site emergency response plan shall be reviewed periodically and, as necessary, be amended to keep it current with new or changing site conditions or information. | |
| (E) An employee alarm system shall be installed in accordance with 29 CFR 1910.165 | |
| (F) Based upon the information available at the time of the emergency, the employer shall evaluate the incident and the site response capabilities and proceed with the appropriate steps to implement the site emergency response plan | II.2.d; II.2.e; III.3.d.(1). |
| 1910.120(q)   Emergency response to hazardous substance releases: | |
| (1) Emergency response plan | III.3.1. |
| (2) Elements of an emergency response plan: | |
| (i) Pre-emergency planning and coordination with outside parties | I.4.f; II.2.b; II.2.c; III.2.b; II.2.c; III.3.b.(4); III.3.d. |
| (ii) Personnel roles, lines of authority, training, and communication | I.4.f; II.2.b; III.2.b; II.2.c; III.3.b.(4); III.3.e.(4). |
| (iii) Emergency recognition and prevention | II.1; III.7. |
| (iv) Safe distances and places of refuge | III.3.b.(3); III.3.d.(2). |
| (v) Site security and control | III.3.d.(2); III.3.e.(2). |
| (vi) Evacuation routes and procedures | II.2.d; III.3.b.(3). |
| (vii) Decontamination procedures | III.3.c.(6). |
| (viii) Emergency medical treatment and response procedures | II.2.d; III.3.c.(7); III.3.e.(1). |
| (ix) Emergency alerting and response procedures | II.2; III.2.a; II.2.f; II.4; III.2; III.2.a; III.2.b; III.2.c; III.3.d. |
| (x) Critique of response and follow-up | II.3; III.4; III.4.a; III.6. |
| (xi) PPE and emergency equipment | III.3.e.(6); III.3.f.(3); III.3.d.(2); III.3.e.(6); III.3.f.(3). |
| (xii) Emergency response plan coordination and integration | III.3.e; III.8. |
| (3) Procedures for handling emergency response: | |
| (i) The senior emergency response official responding to an emergency shall become the individual in charge of a site-specific Incident Command System (ICS). | II.2.b; III.3; III.3.a; III.3.b; III.3.b.(1); III.3.b.(2); III.3.e.(3). |
| (ii) The individual in charge of the ICS shall identify, to the extent possible, all hazardous substances or conditions present and shall address as appropriate site analysis, use of engineering controls, maximum exposure limits, hazardous substance handling procedures, and use of any new technologies. | II.2.c; II.2.d; III.3.c.(3). |
| (iii) Implementation of appropriate emergency operations and use of PPE | II.2.c; II.2.d; II.2.e; III.3.c; III.3.c.(1); III.3.d.(1); III.3.d.(2). |
| (iv) Employees engaged in emergency response and exposed to hazardous substances presenting an inhalation hazard or potential inhalation hazard shall wear positive pressure self-contained breathing apparatus while engaged in emergency response. | II.2.d. |
| (v) The individual in charge of the ICS shall limit the number of emergency response personnel at the emergency site, in those areas of potential or actual exposure to incident or site hazards, to those who are actively performing emergency operations. | III.3.c; III.3.e.(5). |
| (vi) Backup personnel shall stand by with equipment ready to provide assistance or rescue. | II.2.d; III.3.e.(5). |
| (vii) The individual in charge of the ICS shall designate a safety official, who is knowledgeable in the operations being implemented at the emergency response site. | II.2.d; III.3.b.(3). |
| (viii) When activities are judged by the safety official to be an IDLH condition and/or to involve an imminent danger condition, the safety official shall have authority to alter, suspend, or terminate those activities. | III.3.b.(3). |
| (ix) After emergency operations have terminated, the individual in charge of the ICS shall implement appropriate decontamination procedures. | III.3.c.(6). |

Federal Register / Vol. 61, No. 109 / Wednesday, June 5, 1996 / Notices    28663

## ATTACHMENT 3: REGULATORY CROSS-COMPARISON MATRICES—Continued

| | ICP Citation(s) |
|---|---|
| (x) When deemed necessary for meeting the tasks at hand, approved self-contained compressed air breathing apparatus may be used with approved cylinders from other approved self-contained compressed air breathing apparatus provided that such cylinders are of the same capacity and pressure rating. | |
| (4) Skilled support personnel. | |
| (5) Specialist employees. | |
| (6) Training | |
| (7) Trainers. | III.6. |
| (8) Refresher training. | |
| (9) Medical surveillance and consultation. | |
| (10) Chemical protective clothing. | |
| (11) Post-emergency response operations. | |

| EPA's Risk Management Program (40 CFR Part 68) | |
|---|---|
| 68.20–36 Offsite consequence analysis ............................................................ | III.3.d.(1). |
| 68.42 Five-year accident history ................................................................... | III.4.b. |
| 68.50 Hazard review .................................................................................... | III.3.d.(1). |
| 68.60 Incident investigation ......................................................................... | III.4.a |
| 68.67 Process hazards analysis .................................................................. | III.3.d.(1) |
| 68.81 Incident investigation ......................................................................... | III.4.a |
| 68.95(a) Elements of an emergency response program: | |
| (1) Elements of an emergency response plan: | |
| (i) Procedures for informing the public and emergency response agencies about accidental releases. | II.2.a; III.2. |
| (ii) Documentation of proper first-aid and emergency medical treatment necessary to treat accidental human exposures. | III.3.c.(7); III.3.e.(1). |
| (iii) Procedures and measures for emergency response after an accidental release of a regulated substance. | II.1; II.2; II.3; II.4; III.3.a–c. |
| (2) Procedures for the use of emergency response equipment and for its inspection, testing, and maintenance. | III.3.e.(6). |
| (3) Training for all employees in relevant procedures ................................ | III.6. |
| (4) Procedures to review and update the emergency response plan ......... | III.6. |
| 68.95(b) Compliance with other federal contingency plan regulations. | |
| 68.95(c) Coordination with the community emergency response plan. | |

Notes to Attachment 3

[1] Facilities should be aware that most states have been authorized by EPA to implement RCRA contingency planning requirements in place of the federal requirements listed. Thus, in many cases state requirements may not track this matrix. Facilities must coordinate with their respective states to ensure an ICP complies with state RCRA requirements.

[2] Facilities should be aware that most states have been authorized by EPA to implement RCRA contingency planning requirements in place of the federal requirements listed. Thus, in many cases state requirements may not track this matrix. Facilities must coordinate with their respective states to ensure an ICP complies with state RCRA requirements.

[3] Facilities should be aware that most states have been authorized by EPA to implement RCRA contingency planning requirements in place of the federal requirements listed. Thus, in many cases state requirements may not track this matrix. Facilities must coordinate with their respective states to ensure an ICP complies with state RCRA requirements.

[4] Section 264.56 is incorporated by reference at § 264.52(a).

[5] Incorporates by reference § 264.37.

[6] Section 265.56 is incorporated by reference at § 265.52(a).

[7] Incorporates by reference § 285.37.

[8] Section 279.52(b)(6) is incorporated by reference at § 279.52(b)(2)(i).

[9] Incorporates by reference § 279.52(a)(6).

[10] Non-response planning parts of this regulation (e.g., prevention provisions) require a specified format.

[11] If a facility is required to develop a strong oil spill contingency plan under this section, the requirement can be met through the ICP.

[12] The appendix further describes the required elements in 120.20(h). It contains regulatory requirements as well as recommendations.

[13] Specific plan requirements for sections listed under 154.1030(b) are contained in 154.1035(a)–(g).

[14] Note: Sections 154.1045 and 154.1047 contain requirements specific to facilities that handle, store, or transport Group I–IV oils and Group V oils, respectively.

[15] Ibid.

[16] Section 1910.38(a)(3) incorporates 29 CFR 1910.165 by reference.

# About the Author

Thomas M. Socha is the Senior Project Manager at People Technology, Inc., located in Rochester Hills, Michigan. Mr. Socha has a Master of Science in Hazardous Waste Management from Wayne State University, Detroit, Michigan.

# Bibliography

United States Environmental Protection Agency. *Region 5, Oil and Hazardous Substances Integrated Contingency Plan.*

United States Environmental Protection Agency. *Standard Operating Safety Guides.* June 1992

United States Environmental Protection Agency, EPA. Tile 40, Code of Federal Regulations, Parts 112.7(d) and 112.20-.21, Oil *Pollution Prevention Regulation—SPCC and Facility Response Plan Requirements.* 2001 Edition.

United States Environmental Protection Agency, EPA. Tile 40, Code of Federal Regulations, Part 68, *Risk Management Programs Regulation.* 2001 Edition.

United States Environmental Protection Agency, EPA. Tile 40, Code of Federal Regulations, Part 264, Subpart D; Part 265, Subpart D; Part 279, *Resource Conservation and Recovery Act Contingency Planning Requirements.* 2001 Edition

United States Federal Register. *The National Response Team's Integrated Contingency Plan Guidance,* Volume 61, No 109, pg. 28641-28664. June 5, 1996.

United States Department of Labor, OSHA. Tile 29, Code of Federal Regulations, Part 1910.38(a), *Emergency Action Plan Regulation.* 2001 Edition

United States Department of Labor, OSHA. Tile 29, Code of Federal Regulations, Part 1910.119, *Process Safety Standard.* 2001 Edition

United States Department of Labor, OSHA. Tile 29, Code of Federal Regulations, Part 1910.120, *HAZWOPER*. 2001 Edition.

United States Department of Labor, OSHA. Tile 29, Code of Federal Regulations, Part 1910.151, *Medical Services and First aid*. 2001 Edition

United States Department of Transportation, United States Coast Guard (USCG). Tile 33, Code of Federal Regulations, Part 154, Subpart F; *Facility Response Plan Regulation*. 2001 Edition.

United States Department of Transportation, RSPA. Tile 49, Code of Federal Regulations, Part 194, *Pipeline Response Plan Regulation*. 2001 Edition.

# Index

0-595-24781-4

Printed in the United States
99342LV00007B/143/A